NORTH CAROLINA

COOK BOOK

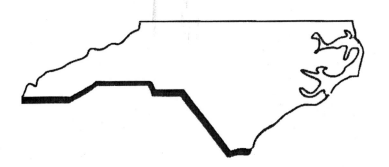

Compiled by
Janice Therese Mancuso

GOLDEN WEST
PUBLISHERS

Acknowledgments

Special thanks to the North Carolina Department of Agriculture and Consumer Services, the North Carolina Pork Council, the North Carolina SweetPotato Commission, Inc., and the North Carolina Apple Growers Association, Inc.

Printed in the United States of America

ISBN 10: 1-885590-42-3
ISBN 13: 978-1-885590-42-8

5th Printing © 2007

Golden West Publishers
4113 N. Longview Ave.
Phoenix, AZ 85014
(602) 265-4392
(800) 658-5830

For free sample recipes from every Golden West cookbook, visit: **www.goldenwestpublishers.com**

Table of Contents

Table of Contents (Continued)

North Carolina

Introduction

North Carolina, which stretches from the Atlantic Ocean to the Appalachian mountain chain, is geographically diverse. Its cuisine is just as exciting. It is a state filled with down home cooking, gourmet restaurants, specialty food markets and barbecue stands—all of which have their own distinctive flavor.

North Carolina Cook Book is filled with family favorites as well as recipes that showcase North Carolina specialty foods. All recipes were contributed by North Carolina residents including homemakers, bed and breakfast owners, regional food producers, food associations, and government agencies.

Enjoy these tastes of North Carolina!

North Carolina Facts

Population — 7.1 million (11th in country)
Size — 52,669 square miles (28th in country)
Capital — Raleigh (established 1792)
Nickname — Tar Heel State
Motto — To Be, Rather Than To Seem
Song — "The Old North State" by Judge William Gaston
Flower — Dogwood
Tree — Pine
Bird — Cardinal
Stone — Emerald
Fish — Channel Bass
Vegetable — Sweet Potato
Reptile — Box Turtle
Mammal — Gray Squirrel
Dog — Plott Hound

Notable Festivals

April: Ham & Yam Festival, Smithfield; ChickenFest, Ahoskie; Pickle Festival, Mt. Olive/Faison

May: Strawberry Festival & Craft Show, Concord

June: Hillsborough Hog Day

July: Piedmont Berry Festival, Dobson; Southeastern NC Watermelon Festival, Fairbluff; NC Watermelon Festival, Murfreesboro

August: Corolla Seafood Festival; Sneads Ferry Annual Shrimp Festival; NC Apple Festival, Hendersonville

September: Ayden Collard Festival; Fruit & Fiber Day, Brevard; Crab & Art Festival, Belhaven; NC Turkey Festival, Raeford; Lincoln County Apple Festival, Lincolnton

October: International Festival, Raleigh; NC Seafood Festival, Morehead City; Peanut Festival, Edenton; Brushy Mountain Apple Festival, North Wilkesboro; Elizabethtown Pork Festival; Livermush Festival, Shelby; NC Oyster Festival, Shallotte

For travel, lodging, and tourism information, visit North Carolina's internet site at: http://www.visitnc.com

Appetizers & Beverages

Cheddar, Crab & Wine Fondue

Duplin Winery—Rose Hill

6 oz. CRABMEAT
20 oz. CHEDDAR CHEESE, shredded
2 Tbsp. ALL-PURPOSE FLOUR
3/4 cup SCUPPERNONG, RIESLING, or your choice of white wine
1/8 tsp. CARAWAY SEEDS

Drain crabmeat well and flake. Toss together cheese and flour. In a saucepan, heat wine until bubbles rise. Over low heat, add cheese mixture to wine, 1/2 cup at a time, stirring after each addition until cheese has melted. Add caraway seeds and crabmeat. Transfer to a fondue pot. Serve with French bread cubes or vegetables for dipping.

Makes 2 1/2 cups.

Shipwrecked Crab

"This is delicious; the guests will eat it up fast! Add green olives at Christmas to make an edible wreath."

T&K Sauces, Inc., Newport

1 lb. CRABMEAT, chopped
1 pkg. (8 oz.) CREAM CHEESE, softened
1 cup SHIPWRECK SAUCE®

On round serving dish, spread cream cheese in circle around dish, leaving center empty. Sprinkle crabmeat over cream cheese. Pour sauce over crab. Serve with your favorite crackers in center.

Lexington

The first silver mine in the United States was the Silver Hill Mine, which opened in 1833 about 10 miles from Lexington.

Blackened Scallops Wrapped with Country Ham

"Country ham and blackening spice add their special flavors to this dish."

Watauga Country Ham—Boone

20 SCALLOPS
20 pieces thinly sliced WATAUGA® COUNTRY HAM
CLARIFIED BUTTER
BLACKENING SPICE

Wrap scallops with ham, secure with toothpicks. In a small bowl, combine butter and blackening spice. Heat cast iron skillet to very hot. Dip scallops in butter mixture. Blacken scallops on both sides, about 4 to 6 minutes.

Sausage Pinwheels

Neese Country Sausage—Greensboro

2 cups ALL-PURPOSE FLOUR	2/3 cup MILK
1 Tbsp. BAKING POWDER	1 lb. NEESE'S® HOT
1 tsp. SALT	SAUSAGE
1/4 cup SHORTENING	grated CHEDDAR CHEESE

Combine flour, baking powder and salt. Cut in shortening and add milk. Turn dough onto a floured surface and roll into an 18 x 12 rectangle. Spread uncooked sausage over dough; sprinkle grated cheese over sausage. Starting at one long end, roll dough tightly (jellyroll fashion), ending with seam on bottom. Cover and refrigerate 1 hour. Slice dough into 1/4-inch slices. Bake at 350° for 20 minutes.

Makes 3 1/2 dozen.

Greensboro

Textile and furniture industries as well as tobacco, electronics and insurance dominate this city's economy. Visit the museum dedicated to the life of legendary NASCAR race driver Richard Petty, or the Guilford Courthouse—scene of a famous civil war battle.

Deviled Eggs

"Web Sauce® can be used for marinating, grilling, or dipping and will add that special zing to your favorite food."

Beverly Carruthers—Web Sauce Foods, Greensboro

8 HARDBOILED EGGS	SALT and PEPPER to taste
4 Tbsp. MAYONNAISE	CAYENNE PEPPER
2 tsp. WEB SAUCE®	or PAPRIKA

Peel eggs; slice in half lengthwise. Remove yolks and mix with mayonnaise, sauce, salt and pepper. Mound yolk mixture in egg halves. Sprinkle with cayenne or paprika.

Carolina Turkey Roll

"Turkey breast replaces seafood in these 'sushi rolls.'"

Carolina Turkeys—Mt. Olive

2 oz. RICE VINEGAR
2 1/2 cups WATER
1 cup RICE WINE or WHITE WINE
SALT and PEPPER to taste
2 cups JASMINE RICE or SUSHI RICE
1 pkg. NORI (roasted seaweed)
1 lb. oil browned CAROLINA® TURKEY BREAST,
     cut into 1/4 x 3-inch strips
2 CUCUMBERS or ZUCCHINI, cored, cut into 1/8 x 3-inch strips
2 CARROTS, peeled, cut into 1/8 x 3-inch strips
WASABI RADISHES
PICKLED GINGER, sliced

In a saucepan, combine vinegar, water, wine and seasonings. Bring to a boil; stir in rice. Simmer, covered, for 20 minutes. Chill. Place 1 sheet of nori on top of a 12-inch sheet of plastic wrap. Spread with 1 cup cooked rice; press down firmly. On one side of rectangle, place two lines each of turkey, cucumber (or zucchini) and carrots. Using the plastic, roll the nori tightly into a cylinder. Remove plastic wrap and cut rolls into 6 pieces. Repeat with remaining ingredients. Place slices on serving plates and garnish with radishes and pickled ginger.

Serves 6-8.

Nacho Dip

Beverly Carruthers—Web Sauce Foods, Greensboro

1 can (8 1/4 oz.) REFRIED BEANS
2 tsp. WEB SAUCE®
1 cup VELVEETA® CHEESE
8 oz. SOUR CREAM

BLACK OLIVES, sliced
SPRING ONIONS, chopped
TORTILLA CHIPS

Mix beans with sauce. Place in center of platter and microwave for about 2 minutes. Melt cheese and pour over bean mixture. Add sour cream; top with olives and onions. Arrange chips around mixture and serve.

Chutney-Ginger Dip

"A chutney dip for vegetables for health conscious party-goers to enjoy."

Ragsdale-Overton Food Traditions, Smithfield

1 cup LIGHT MAYONNAISE
1/4 cup RAGGY-O® MANGO or PEACH CHUTNEY
2 tsp. grated fresh GINGER
1 tsp. grated LIME or LEMON PEEL

Combine all ingredients. Cover and chill. Serve with sliced cucumbers, carrot sticks and other raw vegetables. Also great with chicken nuggets or wingettes.

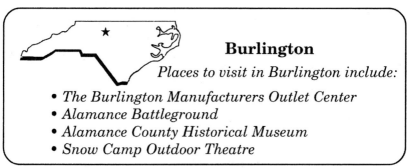

Burlington

Places to visit in Burlington include:

- *The Burlington Manufacturers Outlet Center*
- *Alamance Battleground*
- *Alamance County Historical Museum*
- *Snow Camp Outdoor Theatre*

Spiced Mixed Nuts

"These also make a great gift."

Thomas Gourmet Foods—Greensboro

2 1/2 cups WHOLE ALMONDS, PECANS, and RAW PEANUTS
2 Tbsp. OLIVE OIL
2 Tbsp. THOMAS SAUCE®
1 tsp. CHILI POWDER (add more to taste)
1 tsp. CUMIN
1 Tbsp. SUGAR
1 tsp. SALT

Preheat oven to 300°. Place mixed nuts on a baking pan misted with cooking spray. In a small bowl, combine oil, sauce, chili powder and cumin. Pour over nuts and toss well to coat. Sprinkle with sugar and salt. Bake for 20 minutes, stirring occasionally. Cool and store, covered, at room temperature.

Cheddar Cheese Spread

Thomas Gourmet Foods—Greensboro

2 cups cubed SHARP CHEDDAR CHEESE
1/4 cup softened BUTTER
2 Tbsp. coarsely chopped ONION
1 clove GARLIC
1 1/2 tsp. SEASONED SALT
2 Tbsp. THOMAS SAUCE®
2 med. TOMATOES, peeled, seeded, and coarsely chopped

Place steel blade in food processor and turn on. Drop cubed cheese through feed tube. Turn off processor and add butter, onion, garlic, salt, and sauce. Process until well mixed and fairly smooth. Add tomato and process, leaving small chunks of tomato visible. Oil a mold or line with plastic wrap. Press mixture firmly into mold; cover with plastic wrap and chill. Turn out onto serving plate. Serve with your favorite crackers.

Salsa

"I've made this salsa for years and everyone enjoys it. It also makes a wonderful gift."

Magdalene Comer—Mount Airy

6 qts. TOMATOES, quartered
4 GREEN or RED BELL PEPPERS, chopped
3 med. ONIONS, chopped
5 HOT PEPPERS, chopped
1 1/4 cups VINEGAR
1 cup SUGAR
1/2 cup SALT

In a large stockpot, mix all ingredients together. Simmer for 1 1/2 hours. Pack into sterilized jars and seal according to manufacturer's instructions.

Makes 6-7 quarts.

Mulled Muscadine Cider

"Muscadine grapes have a musky, fruity flavor. Muscadines were one of the first varieties used to make wine in America."

Duplin Winery—Rose Hill

1 qt. MUSCADINE GRAPE JUICE
Dash of ground ALLSPICE
2 (4-inch) sticks CINNAMON
1 LEMON, sliced
1 ORANGE, sliced

Combine all ingredients in a saucepan. Bring to a boil; reduce heat, and simmer 5 minutes. Serve warm.

Makes 1 quart.

Duplin Winery

The Duplin Winery of southeastern North Carolina uses muscadine grapes, which are native to the state, in their muscadine wines and juices. Muscadines are considered to be one of the highest antioxidant content grapes available.

Tamarind Fruit Sauce Dip

"Honey and cayenne pepper produced in North Carolina are in this sauce."

H.S. Sabharwal—Eloras Exquisite Foods, Raleigh

1 pkg. (12 oz.) WHIPPED CREAM CHEESE, softened
1-2 tsp. ELORAS® TAMARIND FRUIT SAUCE

Blend cream cheese and fruit sauce, forming a smooth paste. Refrigerate until ready to serve. Spoon onto serving platter, or serve in bowl. Serve with crackers.

Kool-Aid Punch

"This is a good punch for holidays, but my family loves it all year round."

Stella Hutchens—Yadkinville

2 packs CHERRY or LEMON-LIME KOOL-AID®
2 cups SUGAR
2 qts. warm WATER
1 qt. PINEAPPLE JUICE
1 qt. APPLE JUICE
1 qt. GINGER ALE

Mix all ingredients together (except ginger ale) in a large punch bowl. Add chilled ginger ale when ready to serve.

Did You Know?

Tom Dula (pronounced "Dooley"), a Civil War veteran is buried in Wilkes County. The Kingston Trio immortalized this North Carolina native by recounting the story of his life (and death by hangman's noose) in their song "Tom Dooley".

Jogging in a Jug

"A daily dose of this improves overall health. It also prevents leg cramps and mosquito bites!"

Magdalene Comer—Mount Airy

1 can (12 oz.) frozen APPLE JUICE CONCENTRATE
1 can (12 oz.) frozen GRAPE JUICE CONCENTRATE
9 cups WATER
1 cup APPLE CIDER VINEGAR
1 cup strained HONEY

Mix all in a large glass container. Chill. Drink 2 to 4 ounces daily.

Makes 3 quarts.

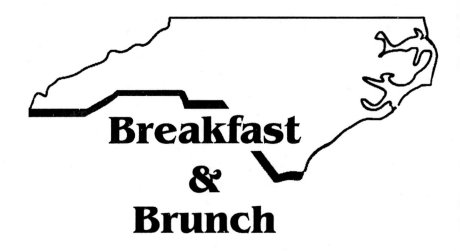

Breakfast & Brunch

Neese's Sausage Quiche

Neese Country Sausage—Greensboro

1 lb. NEESE'S® SAUSAGE
1/2 cup thinly sliced ONION
1/3 cup chopped GREEN BELL PEPPER
1 1/2 cups grated SHARP CHEDDAR CHEESE
1 Tbsp. FLOUR
1 DEEP DISH PIE SHELL
3 EGGS, beaten
1 cup MILK
1 Tbsp. PARSLEY FLAKES
3/4 tsp. SEASONED SALT
1/4 tsp. GARLIC SALT
1/4 tsp. PEPPER

Preheat oven to 375°. In a skillet, cook sausage until browned. Remove and drain on paper towels; crumble when cool. Pour off all but 2 tablespoons of the sausage drippings from the skillet and sauté onion and bell pepper. In a large bowl, combine cheese and flour; stir in crumbled sausage and onion/pepper mixture. Spread in pie shell. Combine remaining ingredients and pour over sausage mixture. Bake for 30 to 40 minutes or until top is browned and filling has set.

Open-Faced Breakfast Sandwich

"In 1943 TW Garner Foods began manufacturing Garners Jams, Jellies & Preserves for the soldiers at Fort Bragg."

TW Garner Food Company—Winston-Salem

1 can (20 oz.) PINEAPPLE SLICES or FRESH PINEAPPLE SLICES
1 pkg. (8 oz.) CREAM CHEESE, softened
1/4 cup GARNERS® PINEAPPLE PRESERVES
8 slices RAISIN BREAD
1/4 cup warmed HONEY

Drain canned pineapple, reserving 1/4 cup juice. Beat cream cheese and juice until light and fluffy; fold in preserves. Toast the raisin bread and spread each slice with the cheese mixture. Top with 1 or 2 slices of pineapple and drizzle with the warm honey.

Makes 8 open-faced sandwiches.

Note: Try this recipe with Garners® Peach Preserves, peach nectar and slices of fresh or canned peaches.

Wine Jelly

Duplin Winery—Rose Hill

3 cups SUGAR
2 cups DRY RED NORTH CAROLINA WINE
1 pkg. (3 oz.) LIQUID PECTIN

Combine sugar and wine in a large saucepan or Dutch oven. Cook over medium heat; stir until sugar dissolves (do not boil). Remove from heat; stir in pectin. Skim off foam with metal spoon. Quickly pour hot jelly into sterilized jars, cover and process.

Makes 4 half-pints of jelly.

French Toast Strata

Eggland's Best—Raleigh

8-10 slices DAY OLD BREAD, cut into cubes
1 cup MILK
1 pkg. (8 oz.) CREAM CHEESE, softened
10 lg. EGGS
1 tsp. CINNAMON
1 tsp. grated NUTMEG
1 tsp. ORANGE EXTRACT or 1 Tbsp. ORANGE LIQUEUR
1 cup BROWN SUGAR
MAPLE SYRUP

Evenly layer bread cubes over the bottom of a greased 9 x 13 baking dish. Blend milk, cream cheese, eggs, spices and orange extract in a blender until well mixed. Pour evenly over bread. Cover and refrigerate overnight. Uncover and bake in a preheated 350° oven for approximately 35 minutes, or until golden brown and knife inserted near center comes out clean. Sprinkle with brown sugar. Serve with warmed maple syrup.

Easy Sausage Scrapple

North Carolina Corn Millers Association

1 cup CORNMEAL
1 tsp. SALT
Dash PEPPER
1 cup COLD WATER

3 cups BOILING WATER
1/2 lb. PORK SAUSAGE,
   cooked, crumbled, drained
2 tsp. shredded GREEN ONION

Combine cornmeal, salt, pepper and cold water. Slowly pour into boiling water, stirring constantly. Cook until thickened, stirring constantly. Cover and continue cooking over low heat about 5 minutes, stirring occasionally. Add pork sausage and onion, mixing well. Pour mixture into a loaf pan which has been rinsed with cold water. Cool slightly; cover and refrigerate several hours or overnight. To serve, cut into 1/2-inch slices and fry on lightly buttered griddle or in skillet until golden brown, about 10 minutes per side.

Serves 6.

Huevos Rancheros

Eggland's Best—Raleigh

2 lg. EGGS	1 Tbsp. SALSA
1 tsp. VINEGAR	1 Tbsp. low fat SOUR CREAM
1 cup BLACK BEAN DIP	1 tsp. chopped fresh CILANTRO
1 oz. baked TORTILLA CHIPS	Fresh CILANTRO SPRIGS

To poach eggs, bring water to a boil in small skillet over high heat; add vinegar and reduce heat to medium-low and maintain a simmer. Gently break eggs into water, being careful not to break yolks. Cover and simmer 5 minutes or to desired firmness. Meanwhile, place bean dip in a small saucepan and heat over medium heat until warm. To serve, spread bean dip in center of serving plate; top with poached eggs and sprinkle with salsa. Arrange tortilla chips around eggs. Add a dollop of sour cream and sprinkle with cilantro. Garnish with cilantro sprigs, if desired. Repeat for additional servings.

Basic Pancakes

Tim Johnson—Cary

1 EGG	2 cups WHOLE-WHEAT
1 1/2 cups MILK	PANCAKE MIX
1/3 cup OIL	

In a large bowl, beat egg slightly. Add milk and oil, blending well. Stir in **Whole-Wheat Pancake Mix** and beat until smooth. Bake on a hot, lightly oiled griddle using about 1/4 cup batter for each pancake.

Makes 8 (4-inch) pancakes.

Whole-Wheat Pancake Mix

8 cups ALL-PURPOSE FLOUR	1/4 cup SUGAR
2 cups WHOLE-WHEAT FLOUR	2 tsp. SALT
1/3 cup BAKING POWDER	2 tsp. ground CINNAMON

In a large bowl combine all ingredients. Can be stored for 5-6 weeks in a covered container in refrigerator or freezer.

Makes 11 cups of pancake mix.

Swiss Brunch Surprise

North Carolina Corn Millers Association

3/4 cup CORNMEAL
3/4 tsp. BAKING SODA
3/4 tsp. SALT
1 1/4 cups BOILING WATER
2 Tbsp. BUTTER

3/4 cup BUTTERMILK
3 EGG YOLKS, slightly beaten
3 EGG WHITES, stiffly beaten
1 cup diced, cooked HAM
2 cups grated SWISS CHEESE

Heat oven to 375°. Grease a 2-quart casserole and place in a pan of hot water to preheat. Blend cornmeal, soda and salt. Slowly add boiling water, stirring until mush is formed. Add butter and cool slightly. Blend in buttermilk and beaten egg yolks. Carefully fold in stiffly-beaten egg whites, ham and cheese. Bake approximately 45 minutes or until knife inserted halfway between center and outside edge comes out clean.

Serves 5-6.

Garden Frittata on Grilled Country Bread

Eggland's Best—Raleigh

3 lg. EGGS
1 Tbsp. chopped fresh BASIL
1 Tbsp. chopped GREEN ONIONS
1 Tbsp. chopped TARRAGON
2 Tbsp. freshly grated ROMANO CHEESE
1 clove GARLIC, minced
2 slices ITALIAN COUNTRY BREAD, buttered and grilled

Mix eggs with all ingredients except garlic and bread. Place garlic in buttered omelet pan and sauté for 30 seconds. Add egg mixture and cook until bottom sets. Place under broiler to set top. Fold in half and place between buttered, grilled bread slices. Cut in half diagonally.

Serves 1.

Country Ham Quiche

"Historically, the country ham was a staple for our agricultural lifestyle. The settlers knew that the ham was one pork item that, when properly cured, could be stored for long periods of time."

Old Waynesboro Country Ham—Goldsboro

4 EGGS
1 cup WHIPPING CREAM
1/2 cup MILK
Dash PEPPER
Pinch of ground NUTMEG
1/3 cup finely grated GRUYÈRE CHEESE
1/3 cup finely grated SWISS CHEESE
1 unbaked 9-inch PIE SHELL
1 cup chopped, cooked OLD WAYNESBORO® COUNTRY HAM

Beat eggs; add cream, milk, pepper, and nutmeg. Blend in cheeses. Line bottom of pie shell with chopped ham. Pour egg and cheese mixture over ham. Place in preheated 350° oven for 1 hour and 15 minutes, or until knife inserted in center comes out clean. Let stand 10 to 15 minutes before slicing.

Serves 5.

Scuppernong Jelly

Duplin Winery—Rose Hill

4 cups SCUPPERNONG GRAPE
    JUICE
2 tsp. LEMON JUICE

1 box (1.75 oz.) SURE-JELL
7 cups SUGAR

Pour both juices into a large saucepan; add Sure-Jell. Bring to a boil, stirring constantly. Add sugar. Bring to a full rolling boil and boil hard for 1 minute, stirring constantly. Remove from heat. Skim off foam with metal spoon and pour at once into prepared jars.

Makes 8 half-pints.

Southern Country Pancakes

House-Autry Mills, Inc.—Newton Grove

1 1/2 cups HOUSE-AUTRY® HUSHPUPPY MIX
1 cup MILK
1 EGG
1 Tbsp. OIL

Combine all ingredients together until just moistened. For each pancake, pour scant 1/4 cup batter into hot, lightly greased griddle. Turn when surface of pancake has large bubbles.

Makes 12 pancakes.

Apricot Conserve

"Serve as you would a preserve on scones, toast, English muffins and other breads."

Gloria T. Rogers—Four Rooster Inn, Tabor City

2 cups DRIED APRICOTS
1 cup DRIED CRANBERRIES
1 can (20 oz.) CRUSHED PINEAPPLE, drained
1 1/2 cups RAISINS
4 cups SUGAR
1 cup chopped ROASTED WALNUTS

In large saucepan, cover and cook apricots over medium heat 15-20 minutes or until tender. In small saucepan, cover and cook cranberries over medium heat 15-20 minutes or until tender. Drain both on paper towels. Place apricots in a bowl and mash with a fork until smooth. Return apricots and cranberries to large saucepan. Add pineapple, raisins and sugar. Bring mixture to boil. Add walnuts. Spoon hot mixture into hot jars, leaving 1/4-inch headspace; wipe jar rims and apply lids. Process in boiling water bath for 15 minutes.

Makes 8 half-pints.

Scuppernong Grape Butter

Duplin Winery—Rose Hill

5 lbs. SCUPPERNONG GRAPES
5 cups SUGAR
1 tsp. ground CLOVES
2 tsp. ground MACE
2 tsp. ground CINNAMON

Wash grapes; drain and remove stems. Plunge grapes into rapidly boiling water to cover; boil 2 minutes. Drain well. Slip off grape skins and grind or chop skins finely, reserving pulp; set skins aside. Place pulp in a heavy saucepan; cook over medium heat 10 minutes or until seeds begin to separate from pulp. Press pulp through a sieve to remove seeds; discard seeds. Return pulp to saucepan; add reserved skins and remaining ingredients. Cook over medium-low heat, stirring constantly, 30 minutes or until mixture thickens. Quickly ladle butter into hot sterilized jars, leaving 1-inch headspace. Cover at once with metal lids and screw bands tight. Process in boiling water bath 5 minutes.

Makes 8 half-pints.

Did You Know?

The Scuppernong grape was originally known as the "Big White Grape." It took its name from Scuppernong Lake near the Albemarle Sound, where it was "officially discovered" in 1755.

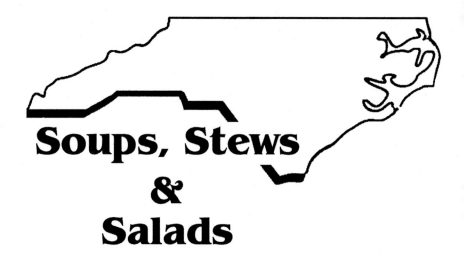

Soups, Stews & Salads

Grandma's Brunswick Stew

"Many a family gathering centered around a big pot of this hearty and economical stew."

Maggie Fulk—King

4 lbs. PORK
2 lbs. PORK LIVER
WATER
2 qts. STEWED TOMATOES
2 cans (15 oz. ea.) WHITE CREAMED CORN
VINEGAR to taste (start with 1/4 cup)
SAGE to taste (start with 1 tsp.)
SALT and PEPPER to taste

In a large Dutch oven cook pork and pork liver until done. Remove pork from bone and chop pork and pork liver to consistency of hamburger. (A food processor works great.) Return pork and liver to the stock left in the pot and add remaining ingredients. Bring to a boil, reduce heat, and simmer for 30 minutes.

Country Kitchen Soup

Tar Heel Kitchen—North Carolina Department of Agriculture and Consumer Services, Raleigh

1 lb. BONELESS PORK, cut into 1/2 inch cubes
1 Tbsp. OIL
1 cup thinly sliced CARROTS
1 cup diced CELERY
1 cup cubed, peeled POTATOES
1 env. BEEFY ONION SOUP MIX
1 can (28 oz.) WHOLE TOMATOES, chopped
4 cups HOT WATER
2 Tbsp. SUGAR
1/2 tsp. PEPPER
1/2 tsp. OREGANO, crushed
1 pkg. (10 oz.) sliced frozen OKRA

In a Dutch oven, brown pork cubes in hot oil. Add carrots, celery and potatoes and cook one minute. Add remaining ingredients except okra. Cover and simmer 1 hour, stirring often. Add okra and cook 15 additional minutes. Serve with crackers or cornbread.

Serves 8.

Chicken Noodle Soup

Anne's Old Fashioned Foods—Ayden

10 strips ANNE'S OLD FASHIONED® FLAT DUMPLINGS
6 cups WATER
2 Tbsp. ANNE'S OLD FASHIONED® CHICKEN BASE
1 can (5 oz.) cooked CHICKEN CHUNKS
SALT and PEPPER to taste

Using a sharp knife, cut dumpling strips into 1/2-inch wide pieces. In a large saucepot bring water and chicken base to a boil. Add strips; cook until tender. Add chicken chunks, salt and pepper. Cook 5 minutes.

Serves 4-6.

Sweet Potato Soup

North Carolina SweetPotato Commission—Smithfield

2 Tbsp. BUTTER
2 Tbsp. finely grated fresh GINGER
3 stalks CELERY, finely chopped
1 lg. ONION, finely chopped
1 Tbsp. CURRY POWDER
1/2 tsp. CINNAMON
1/4 tsp. CAYENNE PEPPER
1/8 tsp. NUTMEG
2 1/2 lbs. SWEET POTATOES, peeled and cut into 1/2-inch cubes
6 cups reduced sodium CHICKEN BROTH
1/2 tsp. dried THYME
1 sm. BAY LEAF
SALT and PEPPER to taste
1/2 cup MILK
SOUR CREAM
ROASTED PEANUTS, chopped

In a large pot over medium heat, melt butter. Add ginger, celery and onion; cook 5 to 7 minutes until soft. Add curry powder, cinnamon, cayenne and nutmeg. Cook 1 minute, stirring constantly. Add sweet potatoes, broth, thyme, bay leaf, salt and pepper. Increase heat to high and bring to a boil. Lower heat to medium and simmer 25 minutes or until sweet potatoes are cooked through. Transfer soup in batches to blender or food processor and purée. Thin soup with milk. Spoon into bowls and garnish with a dollop of sour cream and chopped peanuts.

Serves 12.

Did You Know?

The sweet potato was officially designated the Official State Vegetable of North Carolina by the General Assembly in 1995. North Carolina is the largest producer of sweet potatoes in the nation. The sweet potato is high in vitamins A and C and low in fat. Sweet potatoes were grown in North Carolina before the European colonization of North America.

Chicken Stew

"In the western section of North Carolina, chicken stew reigns supreme. Each year in October, our church has a stew, hayride and marshmallow roast."

Ray Baird—Rural Hall

12 pkgs. (3 lbs. ea.) CHICKEN PIECES
16 (1 1/2 lb. ea.) CHICKEN BREASTS
6 gallons MILK
6 cans (12 oz. ea.) EVAPORATED MILK
4 lbs. MARGARINE
3 Tbsp. POULTRY SEASONING
SALT and PEPPER to taste
2 cups CORNSTARCH
WATER

In a large saucepan, cover chicken pieces and breasts with water and cook until tender. Reserve broth. Cool chicken, remove skin and bones, and refrigerate overnight. Place chicken broth and milk in a large pot and bring to a boil. Cook until chicken flakes and comes apart. Add evaporated milk and margarine and bring back to a boil. Add salt and pepper. Reduce heat and simmer. In a small saucepan, mix cornstarch with enough water to make a paste. Add starch mixture to stew a little at a time to thicken as desired. Serve with crackers.

Serves 60-100.

Hiddenite Emeralds

The largest emerald ever found in North Carolina was 1,438 carats and was found at Hiddenite. The "Carolina Emerald," now owned by Tiffany & Company of New York, was also found at Hiddenite in 1970. When cut to 13.14 carats, the stone was valued at the time at $100,000 and became the largest and finest cut emerald on the continent.

Rabbit Stew

Vaughn Jett—Durham

1 (3 lb.) whole RABBIT, cleaned and dressed
WATER to cover
4 cloves GARLIC, crushed
2 Tbsp. THYME
2 Tbsp. ROSEMARY
1 Tbsp. PARSLEY
1 tsp. SAGE
2 tsp. BLACK PEPPER
2 1/2 lbs. POTATOES, washed & coarsely cubed
2 medium ONIONS, peeled & quartered
1 lb. CARROTS, washed and sliced
1 lb. CABBAGE, sliced
1 can (28 oz.) WHOLE TOMATOES
1 cup PEARL BARLEY
1 cup RED WINE
1/2 lb. frozen PEAS

Place rabbit in a large stockpot and cover with water. Add garlic and all seasonings and cook over medium heat, covered, until meat falls off the bone (about 1 hour). Remove rabbit from stockpot and add potatoes, onions, carrots, cabbage, and canned tomatoes to cooking liquid. Cook, covered, over medium heat for 1/2 hour, adding more water as needed. When rabbit cools, pick meat from bones and add to stockpot. Add barley and wine; cook about 20 minutes or until the barley is tender. Add peas, and cook an additional 5 minutes.

Serves 8 to 10.

Bath

The oldest town in the state is Bath, incorporated in 1705. Bath has many historic buildings and a colorful past including an association with the feared pirate, Blackbeard.

The World's Fastest Brunswick Stew

"This had to be fast. I was a working mother of twins and time and budget were tight."

Susan Johnson—Cary

4 CHICKEN BREASTS
2 cans (10.75 oz ea.) TOMATO SOUP
2 cans (12 oz. ea.) WHITE CORN
1 can (16 oz.) BABY LIMA BEANS
SALT and PEPPER to taste
TABASCO® to taste

Cook chicken breast in water until tender. Debone and shred. Return to broth with soup and vegetables. Simmer for about 1 hour. Add salt, pepper and Tabasco to taste. Serve with pickles and cheese toast.

Serves 6-8.

Tim's Eleven-Bean Soup

"My mountain heritage and memories of the ever-present smell of cooking pinto beans and biscuits led to this recipe."

Tim Johnson—Cary

1 lb. mixture of 11 kinds of BEANS
1/2 cup BARLEY
6 oz. COUNTRY HAM LEAVIN'S
2 Tbsp. GREY POUPON® MUSTARD
WORCHESTERSHIRE SAUCE

Soak beans and barley for 2 days, soaking and rinsing repeatedly. Bring to a boil, cool, bring to a boil, cool; until you're tired of that activity. Add remaining ingredients and cook until beans are tender.

Note: This recipe does not need any salt. If you do add salt, you'll have too much. If you want to reduce the amount of salt already in this soup, add two peeled and halved potatoes.

North Carolina Fruit Salad Supreme

North Carolina Apple Growers Association, Inc.—Edneyville

Juice of 2 LEMONS
1/2 cup PINEAPPLE JUICE
2 Tbsp. FLOUR
1 cup SUGAR
2 EGGS, well beaten
3 BANANAS, sliced
1 cup PECANS, chopped
3 med. NORTH CAROLINA APPLES, peeled and cut in pieces
3 stalks CELERY, chopped
1 can (8 1/4 oz.) PINEAPPLE CHUNKS, drained

Place lemon and pineapple juices, flour, sugar and eggs in a saucepan and cook over medium heat until mixture is thick and clear. Pour into a glass bowl, cover and chill. When ready to serve, place balance of ingredients in a serving bowl and pour lemon mixture over all. Toss to combine.

Egg Salad Spread with Green Tomato Chutney

"A new and exciting taste for an 'old favorite' spread."

Sue H. Overton—Ragsdale-Overton Food Traditions, Smithfield

Chopped HARD-BOILED EGG
RAGGY-O® TOMATO CHUTNEY to moisten
MAYONNAISE to taste
Chopped WALNUTS

Mix all ingredients together to desired consistency. Spread on sandwich bread, biscuit or roll.

Macaroni & Tuna Salad

"Despite the 1933 depression, the Garner family business expanded. Samuel Garner traveled the roads of North Carolina distributing products to restaurants and grocery stores from the back of his station wagon."

TW Garner Food Company—Winston-Salem

1 cup MAYONNAISE
1/4 cup TEXAS PETE® HONEY MUSTARD SAUCE
1 Tbsp. TEXAS PETE® HOT SAUCE
1 pkg. (8 oz.) SHELL or TWIST MACARONI
1 cup cooked fresh or frozen PEAS
2 CARROTS, chopped
1/2 ONION, chopped
1 can (6 1/2 oz.) TUNA, drained
SALT and PEPPER to taste
1 GREEN BELL PEPPER, 1/2 chopped and 1/2 cut into rings

Combine mayonnaise, honey mustard sauce and hot sauce. Mix well and set aside to allow the flavors to blend. Cook the macaroni according to package directions, drain and rinse with cold water. Turn the macaroni into a casserole or serving dish and add the vegetables (except pepper rings) and tuna. Fold in the sauce and add the salt and pepper. Add the pepper rings to the top of the salad. Refrigerate until ready to serve.

Serves 6-8.

Winston-Salem

Pennsylvania Moravians built Salem in 1766. Nearby Winston was founded in 1849 and, thanks to the prosperity of tobacco and textile industries, grew rapidly. The two cities were consolidated in 1913. Here you will find North Carolina School of the Arts, Wake Forest University, Winston-Salem Teacher's College and Salem College.

Lemon, Blueberry & Chicken Salad

Tar Heel Kitchen—North Carolina Department of Agriculture and Consumer Services, Raleigh

2 cups fresh BLUEBERRIES
3/4 cup low-fat LEMON YOGURT
3 Tbsp. reduced-calorie MAYONNAISE
1 tsp. SALT
2 cups chopped CHICKEN
1/2 cup sliced GREEN ONIONS
3/4 cup sliced CELERY
1/2 cup diced sweet RED BELL PEPPER
ENDIVE or other GREENS
LEMON SLICES

Reserve a few blueberries for garnish. In a medium bowl, combine yogurt, mayonnaise and salt. Add remaining blueberries, chicken, green onions, celery, and bell pepper; mix gently. Cover and refrigerate to let flavors blend at least 30 minutes. Serve over endive or other greens garnished with reserved blueberries and lemon slices.

Serves 4.

Sweet Potato Salad

North Carolina SweetPotato Commission—Smithfield

1 lb. SWEET POTATOES, peeled and cut into 1-inch pieces
2 Tbsp. VEGETABLE OIL
1/2 lb. fresh WHOLE GREEN BEANS
1 sm. PURPLE ONION, halved and sliced
1 med clove GARLIC, minced
1 cup WATERCRESS SPRIGS
1 Tbsp. RED WINE VINEGAR
1/2 tsp. SALT
1/4 tsp. freshly ground BLACK PEPPER
PARMESAN CHEESE, shaved

In a large skillet over medium-high heat, sauté sweet potatoes in oil until lightly browned. Add green beans, onion and garlic. Cook until beans are tender-crisp. Remove from heat and stir in remaining ingredients (except cheese). Serve warm, topped with cheese.

Serves 6.

Raggy-O Chicken Salad

"Won best in three categories presented by Our State magazine at the North Carolina Specialty Food Convention in 1998. Prepare a day ahead to blend flavors."

Sue H. Overton—Ragsdale-Overton Food Traditions, Smithfield

3 cups diced, cooked CHICKEN
1/2 cup toasted sliced ALMONDS
4 GREEN ONIONS with tops, chopped
1 can WATER CHESTNUTS, drained
1 cup HELLMAN'S® MAYONNAISE
3 Tbsp. RAGGY-O® PINEAPPLE CHUTNEY
2 tsp. CURRY POWDER
juice of 1 LEMON

Mix chicken, almonds, onions and chestnuts together. Blend remaining ingredients, and stir into chicken mixture. Serve in Bibb lettuce cups.

Pork & Pasta Salad

North Carolina Pork Council—Raleigh

3/4 lb. cooked PORK LOIN
1/2 cup diagonally sliced CARROTS
8 oz. SPINACH FETTUCCINE
1 sm. BERMUDA ONION, sliced and separated into rings
1/4 cup TARRAGON VINEGAR
2 Tbsp. VEGETABLE OIL
1/8 tsp. dried TARRAGON, crushed
1/8 tsp. dried BASIL, crushed

Cut pork into 1/2-inch cubes. Set aside. Place carrots in steamer basket over boiling water and cook for 10-12 minutes or until crisp-tender. Cook fettuccine according to package directions. Rinse well with hot water. In a large bowl combine pork, carrots, fettuccine and onions. In a shaker container combine vinegar, oil, tarragon, and basil; cover and shake well. Pour over fettuccine mixture. Toss gently to coat. Chill 2 to 4 hours. Toss again before serving.

Carolina Blender Slaw

"One of the unsung attributes of 'Eastern North Carolina Barbeque' is the tart and tangy slaw that enhances the flavor of the meat. This is a favorite slaw recipe that can be made in the blender. It is adapted from the slaw that my boyhood memories and tastes still recall."

Roy Baird—Rural Hall

1 large CABBAGE	1/2 tsp. SALT
2 Tbsp. SUGAR	1 tsp. CELERY SEED
2 Tbsp. CIDER VINEGAR	6 Tbsp. MAYONNAISE
1/2 tsp. PEPPER	

Slice cabbage and cut into 1-inch chunks. Fill blender with cabbage chunks; cover with water and blend, in chop or grind mode, until fine. Pour into a large colander. Repeat with remaining cabbage chunks until all is processed. Press out water. Leave cabbage in colander. Mix all remaining ingredients together and add to cabbage in colander. Continue to mix until excess liquid runs through colander, adding more mayonnaise if needed. Cover and refrigerate. Keeps four days.

Watermelon Salad

Tar Heel Kitchen—North Carolina Department of Agriculture and Consumer Services, Raleigh

1 pkg. (3 oz.) FRUIT FLAVORED GELATIN	1/4 tsp. SALT
1-2 Tbsp. LEMON JUICE	1 cup CRUSHED PINEAPPLE
1/2 cup MAYONNAISE	1 cup WATERMELON CUBES

Prepare gelatin according to package directions. Add lemon juice, mayonnaise and salt, blending well. Chill until firm (20-25 min.). Turn into bowl and beat with mixer until fluffy and thick. Fold in pineapple and watermelon. Pour into mold and chill until firm.

Cobb Salad

Mt. Olive Pickle Company—Mt. Olive

1 sm. head ea. CHICORY and ROMAINE LETTUCE, cleaned and
    shredded
1 bunch WATERCRESS
2 whole boneless, skinless CHICKEN BREASTS
1/4 cup PICKLE JUICE
PICKLED PEPPER DRESSING (recipe below)
8 sweet or spicy GHERKINS, diced and divided
2 oz. BLUE CHEESE, crumbled
1 lg. ripe AVOCADO, cut in cubes
2 HARDBOILED EGGS, cut in pieces
2 med. TOMATOES, seeded and cubed
8 slices cooked BACON, crumbled

In a large bowl, toss together chicory and romaine lettuce. Add half the watercress; set aside. In a large skillet over medium-high heat, simmer chicken breasts in pickle juice for 5 to 7 minutes or until no pink juices run when meat is pierced with a knife. Set aside to cool. Toss greens with half of the *Pickled Pepper Dressing* and half of the diced pickles; spread mixture on a large round serving plate. Cut chicken into cubes. Mound cheese in center of greens and arrange chicken, avocado, eggs and tomatoes in a spoke pattern on top of greens. Spoon remaining dressing over salad. Sprinkle bacon and remaining pickles over salad. Garnish with watercress. Refrigerate 15 to 30 minutes.

Serves 6-8.

Pickled Pepper Dressing

1/2 cup OLIVE OIL
1/2 cup chopped FRESH BASIL
2 cloves GARLIC, crushed
3 Tbsp. PARMESAN CHEESE
4 Tbsp. finely chopped SWEET PICKLED RED
    or CHERRY PEPPERS

In a medium bowl, blend together all ingredients with a wire whisk.

Makes 2/3 cup dressing.

Main Dishes

Turkey "Savory Waffle" Sandwich

Carolina Turkeys—Mt. Olive

Spread:
   1/3 cup MAYONNAISE
   1/4 cup prepared BROWN MUSTARD
   1 tsp. freshly ground PEPPER
   1 tsp. LEMON JUICE
8 WAFFLES*
**1 lb. cooked CAROLINA TURKEY BREAST, thinly sliced or
   shaved**
1 TOMATO, thinly sliced
1/4 head LEAF or ICEBERG LETTUCE

In a bowl, combine mayonnaise, mustard, pepper and lemon juice. Mix well. Spread 1 tablespoon of spread on one side of each waffle. Place 4 ounces of turkey on four of the waffles, layer with lettuce and tomato. Top each with the remaining waffles. Insert toothpicks to hold sandwich together and cut into halves or quarters.

*Multi-grain waffles are best.

Pig Pickin'

"A celebration featuring the slow roasting of a dressed pig that is basted with vinegar and crushed hot peppers. The tender meat is then picked (chopped or sliced) off the bone and enjoyed."

Willis Peaden & Jim Elder—North Carolina
State Barbecue Champions

1 (75 to 100 lb.) DRESSED PIG
1/2 lb. SALT
BARBECUE SAUCE (Eastern, Piedmont, or
Western—see pages 40-41)

Split backbone to allow pig to lay flat, being careful not to pierce skin. Trim and discard any excess fat. Sprinkle salt inside cavity. Set pig aside. Place 20 pounds charcoal in pork cooker. Pour 1 quart charcoal lighter fluid over top and ignite. Let burn until charcoal has turned ash-gray. Place heavy gauge wire, about the size of pig, over pork cooker, 13 inches from coals. Place pig flat, skin side up, on wire surface. Close lid of cooker; cook at 225° for 6 hours, using additional lighted coals as needed to maintain temperature in cooker. Place a second piece of wire over pig, sandwiching pig between the 2 layers of wire. Turn pig over, remove wire from top. Insert meat thermometer in thigh; do not touch bone. Baste meat with barbecue sauce; pour sauce in rib cavity to measure 1 inch. Close cooker lid, cook at 225° for 2 hours, until meat thermometer registers 170° and no pink meat is visible when hams and shoulders are cut. Slice or chop meat or allow guests to pull (pick) meat from bones. Serve with barbecue sauce.

Serves 70.

Note: Cooked meat may be frozen for up to three months.

Jan's Baked Rock Fish

"Here's one of my favorites—my wife's traditional recipe for rock fish. She is a native of the Outer Banks—Mann's Harbor."

Tom Jackson—Jackson's Herb Farm, Dunn

1 good sized ROCK FISH (striped bass), whole
FATBACK or BACON
6 med. POTATOES, peeled & coarsely cubed
6 med. ONIONS, peeled & quartered
A lot of BLACK PEPPER, a little SALT
Water to cover vegetables, but to cover only 2/3 of fish

Place fish in pot, slash side diagonally 3 or 4 times. Put fatback in slashes, or cover fish with bacon. Place vegetables around fish. Add pepper, salt and water. Cover and bake at 350° about 1 hour (depends on size of fish & size of vegetable chunks), until done; then uncovered at 375° for about 15 minutes to brown the bacon. When serving, pour juices over fish and vegetables.

The

Outer

Banks

The Outer Banks of North Carolina are a ribbon of barrier islands that protect the eastern coast of the state. Cape Hatteras and Cape Lookout National Seashores can be found here. Visit Ocracoke Island to see wild ponies roaming free, or Roanoke Island where the so-called "Lost Colony" stories abound. According to legend, the pirate Blackbeard was a regular visitor to the Outer Banks during the height of his seafaring career.

E-Z Chicken & Dumplings

"Our delicious chicken base is low in fat and calories."

Anne's Old Fashioned Foods—Ayden

3 qts. WATER
3 Tbsp. ANNE'S OLD FASHIONED® CHICKEN BASE
1/2 stick BUTTER or MARGARINE
1 box (12 oz.) ANNE'S OLD FASHIONED® FLAT DUMPLINGS
1 can (12 oz.) COOKED CHICKEN CHUNKS
FLOUR (optional)
SALT and PEPPER to taste

In a large pot, bring water and chicken base to a boil; add margarine. As broth boils, add 5 to 7 dumpling strips at a time, waiting for broth to return to a boil before adding more dumplings. After all dumplings are in pot, add chicken; cook until dumplings are tender. Add flour to thicken broth if desired. Season to taste.

Serves 4-5.

Chicken Breast Stuffed with Country Ham & Cheese

Watauga Country Ham—Boone

8 CHICKEN BREASTS
10 oz. thinly sliced WATAUGA® COUNTRY HAM
4 oz. shredded COLBY JACK CHEESE
4 oz. SPINACH
FLOUR
BUTTER

Cut pocket into each chicken breast and stuff with ham, cheese and spinach. Dredge breasts in flour. Melt butter in skillet, and brown chicken on both sides. Transfer to a baking dish. Cook at 350° until meat is tender (about 30 minutes).

Pork Roast
with "Peppered" Jelly

North Carolina Pork Council—Raleigh

1 Tbsp. minced fresh GINGER or 1 1/2 tsp. ground GINGER
3 cloves of GARLIC, minced
1 (5 lb.) BONELESS PORK ROAST
1/2 cup of APPLE JELLY
1 1/2 tsp. HOT PEPPER JELLY

Preheat oven to 350°. In a small bowl, mix ginger and garlic and rub over pork. In a separate bowl, mix together apple jelly and hot pepper jelly. Set aside. Place the pork in a shallow roasting pan and roast for 45 minutes. Remove the meat and score in a diamond pattern. Spread the jelly mixture generously over the pork, cover and roast until meat thermometer registers 160°.

Baked Ham
with Honey-Apricot Glaze

1 (10-14 lb.) spiral-sliced, fully-cooked SMOKED HAM
Glaze:
   1 cup HONEY
   1 (6 oz.) can frozen ORANGE JUICE CONCENTRATE, thawed
   1/3 cup SOY SAUCE
   1/3 cup APRICOT JAM
   1/2 tsp. ground NUTMEG
   1/4 tsp. ground CLOVES

Preheat oven to 325°. Place ham on rack in shallow roasting pan. Mix together glaze ingredients in a medium bowl; set aside. Bake ham for 30 minutes; pour glaze over top and continue to bake until ham is heated through, about 1 to 1 1/2 hours.

Serves 14.

North Carolina Pork Barbecue

"North Carolina barbecue sauce recipes are numerous. The sauce used predominately in the East is a clear sauce of vinegar, pepper, and salt mixed in various proportions. Western sauces use ketchup, sugar, and a variety of spices in addition to vinegar and pepper."

North Carolina Pork Council—Raleigh

4 -5 lb. PORK BOSTON BUTT
1/4 cup CIDER VINEGAR
1-2 Tbsp. MOLASSES
BARBECUE SAUCE of choice
(Piedmont, Basic Estern or Western Style—see following)

Place pork in slow cooker; pour vinegar and molasses over top. Slow cook according to cooker directions for 10 hours. Cool, debone, and remove skin and excess fat. When done, chop meat and add barbecue sauce to taste. Serve with additional sauce on the side.

The following sauces are great with any cut of pork!

Piedmont

1 1/2 cups DISTILLED WHITE or CIDER VINEGAR
10 Tbsp. TOMATO KETCHUP
1/2 cup WATER
1/2 tsp. CAYENNE PEPPER
Pinch of crushed RED PEPPER FLAKES
1 Tbsp. SUGAR
SALT to taste
Freshly ground PEPPER to taste

Combine all ingredients in a small saucepan and bring to a simmer. Cook, stirring, until the sugar dissolves. Remove from heat and let stand until cool.

(Continued on next page)

North Carolina Pork Barbecue (continued)

Basic Eastern

1 qt. CIDER VINEGAR
SALT to taste
1 oz. dried RED PEPPER, crushed
BLACK PEPPER to taste

Mix all ingredients well. Set aside to blend.

Western-Style

1 cup TOMATO KETCHUP
1 cup BROWN SUGAR
1/2 cup LEMON JUICE
1/2 stick BUTTER
1/4 cup minced ONION
1 Tsp. LIQUID HOT PEPPER SAUCE
1 Tsp. WORCESTERSHIRE SAUCE

Place all ingredients in a heavy saucepan and bring to a boil. Reduce heat and simmer for 30 minutes.

Country-Style Ribs

"Our Pick 'N Sauce was a 1998 Champion in the North Carolina Battle of the Sauces and received the 1998 Best BBQ Award Winner from Carolina in the Morning WECT-TV-6."

Clear Run Farms—Harrells

1 1/2 lbs. COUNTRY-STYLE RIBS
1/2 cup CLEAR RUN FARMS® PIG PICK 'N SAUCE

Place ribs in a shallow dish and cover with sauce. Marinate overnight in the refrigerator. Remove ribs from sauce and cook on the grill over low heat for approximately 45 minutes, brushing occasionally with sauce.

Serves 2 hearty eaters.

Bell Peppers
with Biscuit Stuffing

"This recipe was given to me by my mother, Fleta Fields Smith, and was made at home on the farm by her mother, Ida Florence Coble Fields. This recipe was usually made in the summer using the fresh tomatoes and peppers that grandmother grew in her garden. There are no exact proportions; the amounts depend upon the number of peppers, tomatoes and leftover biscuits. This recipe will not work with anything else but biscuits."

Jane Smith Hill—Winston-Salem

GREEN or RED BELL PEPPERS
BISCUIT STUFFING

Cut peppers in half; remove core and seeds and blanch for 5 minutes. While cooling, make ***Biscuit Stuffing*** (next page); then stuff each half, filling to the top. Place in a baking dish and bake at 375° until well browned or done to taste. Extra stuffing can be baked plain in greased pans.

Biscuits

3 cups SELF-RISING FLOUR (White Lily®, Dainty Biscuit®, or Daily Bread®)
1/3 cup BUTTER or SHORTENING
1 cup BUTTERMILK or SWEET MILK

Measure flour into a mixing bowl; cut in butter (mixture should resemble coarse corn meal). Make a well in the middle of the flour and add most of buttermilk (or sweet milk). Mix with hands or wooden spoon until dough is evenly moist and cleans the sides of the bowl. Turn dough out on a lightly floured surface and gently round into a ball. Knead lightly until it looks mixed. On a lightly floured surface, gently roll dough from center outward to desired thickness with rolling pin, adding just enough flour to prevent dough from sticking. Cut with biscuit cutter into rounds, dusting the cutter lightly with flour as needed. Place cut biscuits on an ungreased cookie sheet and

(Continued on next page)

Bell Peppers with Biscuit Stuffing (continued)

bake at 450° for 10 minutes or until browned as desired. Cool and crumble.

Biscuit Stuffing

Crumbled BISCUITS
Crisp, fried BACON, crumbled (reserve drippings)
ONIONS, finely chopped
SALT
TOMATOES*, peeled and chopped
WATER or TOMATO JUICE

Place a quantity of crumbled biscuits in a large bowl. The consistency should be fairly coarse, but without large lumps. Add crumbled bacon and some of the drippings. Add onion and salt to taste and enough tomatoes to moisten the biscuits. The consistency should be moist but not soggy; add additional water or tomato juice as needed.

*Canned tomatoes may be used in place of fresh.

Did You Know?

The Plott Hound originated in North Carolina around 1750. Named for Jonathan Plott, who developed the breed, the Plott Hound has a beautiful brindle-colored coat and a spine-tingling, bugle-like call. The Plott Hound was officially adopted as the State Dog in 1989.

Delish Fish Dish

"A quick and easy method of cooking fish to give it a great gourmet taste."

Sue H. Overton—Ragsdale-Overton Food Traditions, Smithfield

2-3 Tbsp. RAGGY-O® PINEAPPLE, PEACH, MANGO or GREEN TOMATO CHUTNEY
1 cup BREAD CRUMBS
GROUPER or RED SNAPPER FILLETS

Mix chutney with bread crumbs. Coat fish fillets with mixture. Bake at 350° for 30 minutes.

Carolina Crab Cakes

House-Autry Mills, Inc.—Newton Grove

2 cups drained CRABMEAT
1/4 cup HOUSE-AUTRY® SEAFOOD BREADER
1 EGG, beaten
1/4 cup MAYONNAISE
2 Tbsp. minced SCALLIONS
1 Tbsp. MUSTARD

Mix all ingredients thoroughly. Shape into 8 patties. Coat with additional breader. Cook in 1/8-inch hot oil for 5 minutes, turning halfway through cooking.

Serves 4.

Raleigh

Founded in 1792 and named for Sir Walter Raleigh, the land for this city was purchased for the sole purpose of it becoming the site of the state capital. The capitol building itself was completed in 1840.

Sweet Potatoes & Ham

North Carolina SweetPotato Commission—Smithfield

1 lb. HAM, sliced
3 med. SWEET POTATOES, sliced
2 Tbsp. BROWN SUGAR
1 cup HOT WATER

Brown ham slightly on both sides and place in a baking dish. Place sliced sweet potatoes over ham and sprinkle with sugar. Deglaze pan with water and pour over sweet potatoes. Cover and bake at 350° until sweet potatoes are tender, about 1 hour. Baste occasionally while cooking. To brown, uncover the last 15 minutes of cooking.

Serves 4.

Chicken & Pastry

"This recipe was passed down from my grandmother to my mother and then to me."

Doris Edwards—Cerro Gordo

1 WHOLE CHICKEN
4 cups sifted FLOUR

2 Tbsp. OIL
1 cup COLD WATER

In a large saucepan, cover chicken with water and boil until meat comes off the bone. Mix flour, oil and water into a stiff dough. Roll out small pieces of pastry until thin and cut into small strips. Cool, then remove bones from cooking liquid. Return to a boil and add pastry strips. Cook for 10-15 minutes, stirring constantly to prevent strips from sticking.

Note: Pastry will roll out thinner if mixed the night before and stored in the refrigerator. Roll pastry on wax paper, sifting additional flour on paper to prevent sticking.

Rock Fish Muddle

"This is a dish my father made each spring when the rock fish spawned in the Roanoke River. He used to fish from the landing at Weldon."

Ray Baird—Rural Hall

1 lb. BACON
2 lbs. ROCK FISH, boned
1 stick MARGARINE
3 large ONIONS, chopped fine
SALT to taste
3/4 tsp. RED PEPPER or 3 crushed dried RED CHILE PEPPERS

In a large skillet, fry the bacon until crisp. Remove bacon from skillet, add margarine to drippings and then the fish; cook fish until it flakes. Add onions and cook 5 minutes over medium heat. Crumble bacon and add with seasonings to skillet. Simmer 2 minutes. Serve with cornbread and cole slaw.

Walnut Crusted Turkey Medallions

"Carolina Turkey is one of the leading turkey producers in the world."

Carolina Turkeys—Mt. Olive

2 1/2 cups chopped WALNUTS
1 cup PLAIN BREAD CRUMBS
1 cup uncooked OATS
1 Tbsp. chopped fresh MINT
1 Tbsp. fresh ground BLACK PEPPER
2 1/4 lbs. raw CAROLINA TURKEY® BREAST,
     cut into 18 (2-oz. ea.), 1/4-inch thick medallions
SEASONED SALT
2 cups ALL-PURPOSE FLOUR
OLIVE OIL
RASPBERRY SAUCE, KEY LIME GLAZE, or MINT SAUCE
1 lb. GOAT CHEESE, crumbled

Combine walnuts, bread crumbs and oats in blender. Grind into a coarse meal. Add mint and pepper; pulse until blended. Set aside. Sprinkle turkey with salt, dredge in flour and then nut meal; pressing meal solidly into place. Sauté turkey in olive oil in preheated skillet over medium heat until golden brown. To serve, place three medallions on pool of sauce on each serving plate; garnish with goat cheese.

Serves 6.

North Carolina Turkeys

North Carolina produces close to 54 million turkeys totaling nearly 1.4 billion pounds annually, more turkeys than any other state in the nation.

Broiled Catfish

Carolina Classics Catfish—Ayden

2 Tbsp. SALAD OIL
Juice of 1 LEMON
CRACKED PEPPER and SALT to taste
4 CLASSICS® CATFISH FILLETS
1 Tbsp. BUTTER or MARGARINE
1 LEMON, sliced
PARSLEY

Combine oil, lemon juice, pepper and salt. Season fillets by rubbing with the oil mixture. Place fillets in a greased baking pan. Dot each fillet with equal amounts of butter. Top with lemon slices. Broil for 10 minutes or until fish is opaque and flaky. Garnish with parsley.

Serves 2.

Ham, Macaroni & Cheese

"Country ham is a traditional food for North Carolinians."

Old Waynesboro Country Ham—Goldsboro

3/4 cup finely chopped, cooked OLD WAYNESBORO®
    COUNTRY HAM
1/4 cup chopped ONIONS
2 Tbsp. BUTTER
1 can (10.75 oz.) CREAM OF MUSHROOM SOUP
1/2 cup MILK
1 cup shredded SHARP CHEDDAR CHEESE
2 cups cooked MACARONI
1/4 cup seasoned STUFFING MIX

Lightly brown ham and onions in butter. Stir in soup, milk, and 3/4 cup cheese. Heat until cheese melts, stirring often. Blend ham mixture and macaroni; pour into buttered 1 1/2-quart casserole dish. Sprinkle with remaining cheese and stuffing mix. Bake in a 350° oven 30 minutes or until nicely browned and bubbling.

Serves 4.

Stuffed Trout

Watauga Country Ham—Boone

2 med. ONIONS, diced
2 Tbsp. chopped GARLIC
2 Tbsp. BUTTER or MARGARINE
6 GRANNY SMITH APPLES, diced
2 cups diced WATAUGA® COUNTRY HAM
2 cups BREAD CRUMBS
2 cups chopped TOASTED PECANS
3 EGGS, beaten
1 Tbsp. SALT
2 tsp. PEPPER
1/2 cup diced fresh OREGANO
1/4 cup diced fresh THYME
6 WHOLE TROUT (about 12 oz. ea.)

Sauté onions and garlic in butter until translucent; add apples and sauté about 2 minutes. Transfer to a large mixing bowl. In the same pan, sauté ham until tender. Add ham, bread crumbs, pecans, eggs, and seasonings to onion mixture, mixing well. Stuff trout with mixture. Place in a buttered baking dish and bake at 400° for 15 to 20 minutes.

Serves 6.

Catfish Veracruz

Carolina Classics Catfish—Ayden

4 CLASSICS® CATFISH FILLETS   Sliced BLACK OLIVES
1 cup PICANTE SAUCE or SALSA   AVOCADO SLICES

Place fillets in an ovenproof shallow dish. Pour picante sauce over fillets; place olives on top. Bake in a preheated 400° oven for 10 minutes or until fish is flaky and opaque. Garnish with avocado slices.

Serves 2.

Shrimp & Grits

"This recipe is a combination of several recipes. It was given to me by my sister, Ginger J. Padgett."

Amy J. Attaway—Berkley Manor Bed & Breakfast, Ocracoke

1 Tbsp. HORSERADISH
1/4 cup KETCHUP
1 tsp. LEMON JUICE
2 oz. CREAM CHEESE
JALAPEÑO PEPPERS, finely chopped, to taste
12 lg. SHRIMP, peeled and deveined
6 strips BACON
2 cups HALF & HALF
2 cups MILK
2 Tbsp. BUTTER
1 cup quick GRITS
SALT and PEPPER to taste
1 cup shredded SHARP CHEDDAR CHEESE
1/3 cup grated fresh PARMESAN CHEESE

In a small bowl, mix the horseradish, ketchup and lemon juice. Refrigerate until ready to serve. In another small bowl, thoroughly mix cream cheese and desired amount of jalapeño peppers. Place in a plastic bag and snip off a very tiny corner. Butterfly the shrimp and lay open. Pipe a narrow bead of the cream cheese mixture into the center of each shrimp. Carefully close the shrimp being careful not to squeeze out the cream cheese. Cut the bacon strips in half so that you have twelve strips (about 4 inches long). Wrap one strip of bacon around the middle of each of the shrimp and secure with toothpicks. Place the shrimp on a broiler pan and broil (or bake at 500°). Cook shrimp 2-3 minutes per side. Meanwhile, put half & half, milk and butter in a large heavy-bottomed stock pot. Bring to a boil. Slowly add the grits, stirring while adding. Reduce heat and simmer until liquid is absorbed. Remove from heat and add salt and pepper and cheddar cheese, stirring to distribute. Divide grits between two soup bowls, sprinkle with Parmesan cheese and top with six shrimp each. Garnish with horseradish sauce.

Serves 2.

Eloras Tamarind Shrimp

"This recipe also works well with pork or chicken."

H.S. Sabharwal—Eloras Exquisite Foods, Raleigh

1 sm. ONION, chopped
2 cloves GARLIC, crushed
1 Tbsp. CANOLA OIL
1 lb. SHRIMP, peeled and deveined
1-2 Tbsp. ELORAS® TAMARIND FRUIT SAUCE
GREEN or RED CHILES to taste
SALT to taste

Stir fry onion and garlic in oil until translucent. Add shrimp and cook until heated through. Add sauce, chiles, and salt. Cook, stirring often, for 3 to 4 minutes. Serve with rice or bread.

Chicken Casserole

"I never have leftovers when I take this to family reunions, parties, or church events."

Gretchen Rhodes—Madison

4 CHICKEN BREASTS
1 can (10.75 oz.) CREAM OF CHICKEN or CELERY SOUP
1 can (10.75 oz.) CREAM OF MUSHROOM SOUP
1 1/4 cups MILK
1 stick MARGARINE
1 pkg. (16 oz.) PEPPERIDGE FARM® DRESSING

In a large saucepan, cover chicken breasts with water and boil until tender. Reserve broth. Cool breasts and remove bones. Cut into bite-size pieces. Place chicken in a 9 x 13 baking dish. In a large bowl, combine soups, milk and 1 cup of reserved chicken broth. Mix well. Melt margarine and blend into dressing mix. Pour soup mixture over chicken and stir. Sprinkle top with dressing. Bake at 350° until brown and bubbly.

Animal John's Shrimp

"This vinegar-based sauce, a 1998 North Carolina Battle of the Sauces 2nd Runner Up, is made to enhance the flavor of all meats, seafood and vegetables! This is why we call it all-purpose; it's good on everything!"

Carrie Riggs & John Riggs—Animal John's Southern Products,
Oriental

2-3 lbs. SHRIMP, cleaned
WATER
Handful of SALT
1 jar (17 oz.) ANIMAL JOHN'S® ALL-PURPOSE
    SOUTHERN SAUCE

Place shrimp in a bowl; cover with water. Add salt, stir, then let sit for about 10 minutes. Wash shrimp with cold water and cook.

To grill: Place shrimp on skewers or lay on grill. Brush with sauce and cook until done. You can marinate the shrimp but not for more than 10 minutes.

On stovetop: Pour some of the sauce in the bottom of a saucepan and heat until it just starts to bubble. Add shrimp and stir until shrimp are cooked. Remove shrimp from saucepan, and place in serving bowl. Continue to cook sauce until reduced to desired consistency. Once thickened, pour over cooked shrimp and allow to sit for 2 minutes before serving.

Asheville

Surrounded by the Great Smoky and Blue Ridge Mountains, Asheville is divided by two rivers, the Swannanoa and the French Broad. The Blue Ridge Parkway, US 74 and I-40 all converge within the boundaries of this city that was first settled in 1794.

Andrea's Meatloaf

Andrea Neese—Greensboro

2 EGGS
1 cup MILK
2/3 cup BREAD CRUMBS
1/2 cup chopped ONION
2 1/2 Tbsp. PARSLEY
1 tsp. SALT
1/2 tsp. SAGE

1/4 tsp. PEPPER
1 lb. NEESE'S® SAUSAGE
   (regular, hot, or sage)
1 lb. GROUND CHUCK
1/2 cup KETCHUP
4 Tbsp. BROWN SUGAR

Combine eggs and milk; stir in bread crumbs, onion, parsley, salt, sage and pepper. Add sausage and beef; mix well. Pat into a 6-cup ring mold. Unmold onto a shallow baking pan. Bake at 350° for 1 hour. Spoon off excess grease. Combine ketchup and brown sugar; spread over meatloaf. Return to oven for 10 minutes.

Serves 4-6.

Oven Fried Chicken

"In 1929, Thad W. Garner purchased a small barbecue stand and a handwritten recipe for barbecue sauce. When customers requested a spicier sauce, red pepper was added and Texas Pete® Hot Sauce was born!"

TW Garner Food Company—Winston-Salem

1 cup BUTTERMILK
1 bottle (12 oz.) TEXAS PETE® HOT SAUCE
SALT and PEPPER to taste
1 FRYING CHICKEN, cut up
2 cups crushed CORN FLAKES
2 Tbsp. MARGARINE

In a large bowl, combine buttermilk, hot sauce, salt and pepper. Add chicken. Cover, and marinate overnight. When ready to cook, remove from marinade, sprinkle skin side with corn flakes and pat on. Melt margarine in baking pan and add chicken pieces, flake side up. Bake at 375° for 1 hour or until juices run clear.

Serves 6.

Grandview
Marinated Pork Roast

"To save time, buy extra gingerroot; grate and freeze in one-ounce portions."

Linda P. Arnold—Grandview Lodge, Waynesville

1 (2 1/2-3 lb.) PORK LOIN ROAST	1 oz. GINGERROOT
1 tsp. DRY MUSTARD	3/4 cup DRY SHERRY
1 tsp. dried THYME LEAVES	3/4 cup SOY SAUCE
3 cloves GARLIC, peeled	

Put pork loin in a shallow pan, fat side up. Mix the mustard and thyme together and rub into the fat. Using a food processor fitted with steel blade, drop the garlic and gingerroot into the chute with the motor running and chop finely; add sherry and soy sauce. Pulse machine a few times. Pour marinade over meat; cover and refrigerate at least 6 hours (preferably 12 hours), turning meat 2-3 times. Remove meat from marinade. Strain marinade into a small saucepan, and place meat and strained solids in a shallow roasting pan. Roast in preheated 325° oven to an internal temperature of 140° (about 1 hour and 15 minutes). Meanwhile, heat the strained marinade to boiling, skimming as necessary. Remove from heat and set aside. When pork loin is ready, remove from oven, cover meat and pan securely and keep in a warm place for 30 minutes. Add accumulated pan juices to marinade and boil down to thicken, removing fat from surface. Slice roast thinly; place on heated platter and pour sauce over top.

Serves 6-8.

Did You Know?

Three North Carolina Tar Heels became president and led the nation through times of war, reconstruction, and expansion: Andrew Jackson, Andrew Johnson and James K. Polk. Another Tar Heel, Zebulon Baird Vance was known as North Carolina's "States Righter" Civil War governor. Vance also served 15 years as a U. S. Senator.

Venison & Potatoes with Greens

"I had some deer meat and these ingredients in my refrigerator, so I developed this recipe."

Vaughn Jett—Durham

2 Tbsp. OLIVE OIL
2 lbs. POTATOES, sliced thin
2 cloves GARLIC, minced
1 lb. VENISON, sliced thin
1 ONION, chopped
1 GREEN BELL PEPPER, chopped
1 small YELLOW SQUASH, sliced
SALT and PEPPER to taste
KALE or COLLARD GREENS, washed

Heat oil in a large skillet over medium-high heat; add potatoes and garlic; cook for 10 minutes, stirring occasionally. Add remaining ingredients except greens. Cook, stirring frequently, until meat is browned and vegetables are tender (about 15 minutes). Top with a layer of greens, cover pan with lid and cook for about 2 minutes, until greens are wilted.

Serves 4.

Classics Cornbread Catfish

Carolina Classics Catfish—Ayden

4 CLASSICS® CATFISH FILLETS
1/2 cup CORNMEAL
1/4 cup COOKING or OLIVE OIL
SALT and PEPPER to taste

Coat fillets with oil then dredge with cornmeal and season with salt and pepper. Place fillets in a greased ovenproof dish. Bake for 10 minutes at 400°.

Serves 2.

Side Dishes

Sweet Potato Casserole

"This recipe was originated by my grandmother and passed down to our generation. It freezes well."

Doris Lewis—Winston-Salem

3 cups mashed SWEET POTATOES
1 cup SUGAR
2 EGGS, beaten
1/2 cup MILK
1/2 tsp. VANILLA
1 stick BUTTER, melted
1 cup BROWN SUGAR
1/2 cup FLOUR
1 cup chopped PECANS or WALNUTS

Combine sweet potatoes and sugar. Mix well. Add eggs, milk and vanilla and half of the melted butter. Place mixture in a greased casserole dish. Mix brown sugar, flour and nuts. Add remaining melted butter. Mix well. Spoon topping over sweet potato mixture. Bake at 350° for 35 minutes.

Uptown Squash

Tar Heel Kitchen—North Carolina Department of Agriculture and Consumer Services, Raleigh

4 cups sliced SQUASH
1/2 cup chopped ONION
1/2 cup WATER
1 pkg. (8 oz.) low-fat SOUR CREAM
1/2 tsp. SALT
1/4 tsp. PEPPER
1/4 tsp. dried BASIL
1 cup SOFT BREAD CRUMBS
1/2 cup shredded CHEDDAR CHEESE
1/4 cup BUTTER
1/2 tsp. PAPRIKA
8 slices BACON, cooked and crumbled

Cook squash and onion in 1/2 cup boiling water until tender; drain and mash. Combine squash, sour cream, salt, pepper, and basil; pour into a greased 2-quart casserole. Combine bread crumbs, cheese, butter, and paprika; sprinkle over squash mixture. Top with crumbled bacon. Bake at 300° for 20 minutes.

Serves 6.

Roasted Red Potatoes

"This is a 'must try' recipe."

Dixie Trail Farms, Inc.—Wilmington

2 lbs. RED POTATOES, cut in half
4 to 8 oz. MELTED BUTTER, MARGARINE or OLIVE OIL
3 to 4 Tbsp. DIXIE TRAIL FARMS® SOUTHERN SIGNATURE™ BUTTER, MARGARINE or OLIVE OIL

Place potatoes in a roasting pan. Coat potatoes with butter and sprinkle liberally with Special Spice. Bake at 350° for 50 minutes. Top each potato with additional butter and bake for another 15 minutes.

Baked Tangy Tomatoes

Tar Heel Kitchen—North Carolina Department of Agriculture and
Consumer Services, Raleigh

4 lg. TOMATOES
2 Tbsp. chopped GREEN BELL
   PEPPER
2 Tbsp. chopped CELERY
1 Tbsp. chopped ONION

1 Tbsp. PREPARED MUSTARD
1/4 tsp. SALT
2/3 cup SOFT BREAD CRUMBS
2 Tbsp. melted BUTTER

Cut tomatoes in half crosswise. Scoop out pulp, leaving shells intact. Chop tomato pulp and combine with bell pepper, celery, onion, mustard and salt; stir well. Spoon into tomato shells, and place in a 9 x 13 baking dish. Combine bread crumbs and butter; sprinkle over tops of tomatoes. Bake at 350° for 25 to 30 minutes.

Serves 8.

Wilmington

Wilmington was the Colonial capital in 1743 and the scene of Stamp Act resistance in 1765. This city is the principal deepwater port of North Carolina.

Hot Dog Chili

Carolina Treet, Inc.—Wilmington

1 lb. GROUND BEEF
2 cups WATER
1/2 cup CAROLINA TREET® BARBECUE SAUCE
HOT DOGS

Brown ground beef and drain excess fat. Add water and sauce to meat and bring to a boil. Reduce heat and simmer until water has evaporated and chili has reached desired thickness. Serve over top of hot dogs.

Serves 4-6.

Tomatoes & Okra

Tar Heel Kitchen—North Carolina Department of Agriculture and
Consumer Services, Raleigh

3 slices BACON
4 cups sliced OKRA, 1/2-inch thick
1 med. GREEN BELL PEPPER, finely chopped
1 med. ONION, chopped
2 cloves GARLIC, minced
4 lg. TOMATOES, peeled and chopped
SALT and PEPPER to taste

Fry bacon until crisp. Remove from fat. Cook okra in bacon
drippings. Add green pepper, onion, and garlic to drippings; stir
in tomatoes and crumbled bacon. Add salt and pepper to taste.
Cover skillet and cook another 15 minutes.

Serves 8.

Scalloped Tomatoes

Tar Heel Kitchen—North Carolina Department of Agriculture and
Consumer Services, Raleigh

6 lg. TOMATOES
1 Tbsp. grated ONION
1 1/2 cups SOFT BREAD CRUMBS
1/4 cup melted BUTTER

Peel tomatoes and cut in quarters. Place in a saucepan and
mash slightly to press out some of the juice. Cook over very low
heat (about 10 minutes), stirring constantly. Add grated onion.
In a 10-quart casserole dish, alternate layers of tomatoes and
bread crumbs. Add butter and bake at 375° for 20 to 30 minutes.

Serves 4-6.

Oven Baked Steak Fries

Thomas Gourmet Foods—Greensboro

1 lb. BAKING POTATOES
1/4 cup THOMAS SAUCE®
1 Tbsp. OLIVE or VEGETABLE OIL
KOSHER SALT

Wash and scrub potatoes. Cut in half lengthwise, then cut each half into 4 or 5 wedges. Soak for 30 minutes in cold water, then dry. In a bowl, mix sauce with oil. Roll the potatoes in the mixture and place on a foil-lined cookie sheet. Sprinkle with salt and bake in a preheated 400° oven for 35 to 45 minutes until tender and browned.

Charlotte

Named for German-born Queen Charlotte, wife of England's King George III, this city is sometimes referred to as Queen City. It is also known as The City of Trees because of the many willow oaks that line its streets.

Fried Green Tomatoes

Tar Heel Kitchen— North Carolina Department of Agriculture and Consumer Services, Raleigh

4 medium GREEN TOMATOES, cut into 1/4-inch slices
1/2 cup CORNMEAL
VEGETABLE OIL
1/4 tsp. SUGAR
SALT and PEPPER to taste

Dredge tomatoes in cornmeal. Fry tomato slices in hot oil in a skillet until browned, turning once. Drain well on paper towels. Sprinkle tomato slices with sugar, salt, and pepper. Serve hot.

Serves 6.

Cashew-Chutney Rice

"For those who want to cut back on meat, this is a wonderful alternative. Also a terrific dish to serve with seafood."

Sue H. Overton—Ragsdale-Overton Food Traditions, Smithfield

1 cup diced CELERY
3/4 cup diced ONION
6 Tbsp. BUTTER or MARGARINE
5 cups CHICKEN BROTH
2 cups LONG-GRAIN RICE
1 cup UNSALTED CASHEWS
2 Tbsp. RAGGY-O® CHUTNEY, any flavor
SALT and PEPPER to taste

Sauté celery and onion in butter. Add chicken broth and bring to a boil. Place rice, cashews and chutney in a 9 x 13 baking dish. Pour broth mixture over rice. Add salt and pepper. Bake at 350° for 45 to 60 minutes.

Tomato Pie

Tar Heel Kitchen—North Carolina Department of Agriculture and Consumer Services, Raleigh

1 (9-inch) DEEP DISH PIE CRUST
6 lg. TOMATOES
2/3 to 3/4 cup MAYONNAISE
2/3 cup grated PARMESAN CHEESE
2-3 Tbsp. chopped fresh BASIL
1-2 Tbsp. chopped PARSLEY
crushed SALTINE CRACKERS

Bake pie crust until golden brown. Peel and slice (or chop) tomatoes and let drain in a colander for 30 minutes. Mix mayonnaise with Parmesan cheese. Toss tomatoes, basil, and parsley. Place tomatoes in pie crust. Spread mayonnaise and cheese mixture over the top. Sprinkle with cracker crumbs. Bake at 375° for 45 to 50 minutes.

Serves 8.

Mom Blevins'
Boston Baked Beans

"I can still remember the delightful smell of these beans cooking as I came home from school on a cold wintry day. Since my mother used a wood cook stove, she would let the beans cook all afternoon. We lived on a small farm in Ashe County and grew most everything we ate. We milked cows, so we had our own fresh milk, buttermilk and butter. We grew corn, which was ground into meal for our cornbread. This recipe was published in a local cook booklet that was put out by the Ashe Services for Aging in 1981. These beans were served with cornbread and cold milk."

Mannon Blevins Eldreth—West Jefferson

2 lbs. PINTO BEANS (cooked as you like them)
5 or 6 large ONIONS (the stronger the better)
2 qts. CANNED TOMATOES, drained (reserve juice)
BACON SLICES
2/3 cup MOLASSES
SALT and PEPPER to taste (needs lots of black pepper)

Drain the pinto beans, reserving the cooking liquid. Spoon a layer of the drained beans in a very large pot that will fit in your oven. Layer thickly sliced onion (the more the merrier), drained canned tomatoes, and sliced bacon. Keep layering beans, onions, tomatoes and bacon to fill the pot. Mix molasses, salt and pepper and drained tomato juice and add to pot to cover the top of the bean mixture. If you don't have enough tomato juice, use some of the bean cooking liquid. Bake, uncovered, at 350° for 2 hours or until liquid is cooked down somewhat.

Did You Know?

In 1629, King Charles I of England created, as a province, all the land from Albermarle Sound on the north to the St. John's River on the south. He directed that this province be called Carolina (from the word Carolus, the Latin form of Charles). When Carolina was divided in 1710, the states of North and South Carolina were formed.

Sorta Baked Beans & Sorta Chili

Carolina Treet, Inc.—Wilmington

1 lb. GROUND BEEF
1/2 med. GREEN BELL
   PEPPER, chopped
1/2 cup CAROLINA TREET®
   BARBECUE SAUCE

1 lg. ONION, chopped
1/2 cup TOMATO KETCHUP
1/4 cup BROWN SUGAR
1 can (31 oz.) PORK 'N' BEANS
SALT and PEPPER to taste

In a skillet, cook beef until brown; drain. Mix all ingredients well and bake in casserole dish at 350° for 35 minutes.

Fayetteville

Located at the head of navigation on the Cape Fear River, Fayetteville is the state's most inland port. Fayetteville's economic mainstays are Fort Bragg, one of America's most important military bases and Pope Air Force Base.

Stuffed Baked Sweet Potatoes

North Carolina SweetPotato Commission—Smithfield

6 med. SWEET POTATOES
1/2 cup ORANGE JUICE
3 Tbsp. MARGARINE
1 tsp. SALT

1 can (8 oz.) CRUSHED
   PINEAPPLE, drained
1/2 cup chopped PECANS

Bake sweet potatoes at 375° for 1 hour or until tender. Cut a 1-inch lengthwise strip from top of each sweet potato; carefully scoop pulp from shell. In a large bowl, combine sweet potato pulp, orange juice, margarine and salt; beat until fluffy. Stir in pineapple. Stuff shells with sweet potato mixture and sprinkle with pecans. Bake at 375° for 10 minutes.

Hushpuppy Fritters

House-Autry Mills, Inc.—Newton Grove

1 cup House-Autry® HUSHPUPPY MIX
1/2 cup MILK
1 EGG
1 cup CORN

Combine hushpuppy mix, milk and egg, mixing until well blended. Let stand 5 minutes. Stir in corn. Drop by level tablespoonfuls into 375° oil. Cook 2 to 3 minutes, or until deep golden brown.

Makes 24 fritters.

Note: For variations, use chopped ham, cooked shrimp or crumbled bacon in place of corn.

Did You Know?

Hushpuppies are small cornmeal dumplings that are deep fried and served hot. They are said to have been created by Southern cooks to keep their dogs from begging.

Glazed Sweet Potatoes

North Carolina SweetPotato Commission—Smithfield

1 Tbsp. plus 1 tsp. MARGARINE   **1 1/4 tsp ground CINNAMON**
1 Tbsp. plus 1 tsp. unsweetened   **2 med. SWEET POTATOES,**
ORANGE JUICE   **peeled**

Slice each sweet potatoe lengthwise into 8 wedges. Place margarine in an 8-inch square baking dish; microwave at HIGH for 30 seconds or until melted. Stir in orange juice and cinnamon; add potatoes, tossing to coat. Cover with wax paper. Microwave at HIGH for 6-8 minutes or until tender, stirring and turning dish once during cooking.

Corn Pudding

"This recipe is my mother's and dates back many generations. Growing up on a farm in North Carolina meant growing up with summer sweet corn. There is a certain nostalgia associated with the rhythmic sound of fresh corn being cut off the cob. It is possible to make this recipe with frozen shoe peg white corn, but never with canned corn."

Linda P. Arnold—Grandview Lodge, Waynesville

2 EGGS
1/2 to 3/4 cup SUGAR
2 Tbsp. FLOUR
4 cups SWEET CORN
1/2 to 3/4 cups MILK
1/2 cup BUTTER or MARGARINE, melted

In a medium size mixing bowl, beat eggs with sugar and flour. Add corn and milk. Stir in melted butter. Pour into a greased 1 1/2 quart baking pan. Bake at 325° for 35 to 45 minutes or until pudding is set and browned on top.

Serves 6-8.

French Fried Pickles

Mt. Olive Pickle Company—Mt. Olive

SALAD OIL
1 EGG, lightly beaten
3 Tbsp. MILK
1 Tbsp. PICKLE LIQUID (dill or sweet)
1/3 cup PANCAKE MIX
1 cup PICKLE SLICES, well drained (dill or sweet cucumber)

Heat one inch of salad oil in skillet or electric skillet to 360° on deep-fat thermometer. Place egg in a small mixing bowl; stir in milk and pickle liquid. Add pancake mix; stir until smooth. Dip pickle slices, one at a time, into batter. Fry in oil 1 to 2 minutes until lightly browned. Remove with slotted spoon and drain on paper towels.

Makes about 2 1/2 dozen.

Squashpuppies

"I combined two North Carolina favorites, hushpuppies and squash, and gave it a new twist with our Pantego Plantation Breader®, a trophy winner from the 1997 Fancy Food Show in New York."

Dianne L. Bowen—Pantego Plantation Gourmet Foods, Pantego

1 pkg. (10 oz.) frozen YELLOW SQUASH
1 lg. EGG, beaten
1/2 cup BUTTERMILK
1 sm. ONION, finely chopped
3/4 cup PANTEGO PLANTATION BREADER®
2 Tbsp. WHITE CORNMEAL
1/4 cup SELF-RISING FLOUR
1/2 cup grated EXTRA SHARP CHEDDAR CHEESE
Freshly grated PEPPER to taste
SALT to taste

Thaw frozen squash and drain off excess water. Process in food processor. Combine squash with remaining ingredients. Heat oil to 360°. Drop squash mixture, 1 teaspoon at a time, in hot oil. Fry 5 minutes or until golden brown. Drain on paper towels. Makes about 3 dozen squashpuppies.

Durham

Once known as "tobacco town", Durham is now known as the "City of Medicine." Duke University and five other major hospitals are located in this region, Durham is known for its excellence in medicine, education, research and industry.

Fried Corn

"My grandmother grew her own corn, and I have precious memories of watching her, my mother, and my aunt cut the corn from the cob under the big shade trees. Grandmother would cook a large frying pan full of corn. It smelled and tasted delicious. Every time I fix this recipe, I think of her."

Margaret A. Thomas—Peachland

4 slices of FATBACK
4 to 6 cups fresh white SILVER QUEEN CORN
3 Tbsp. MARGARINE
SALT and PEPPER to taste
3 1/2 cups WATER
3 Tbsp. self-rising FLOUR

Place fatback in a large frying pan. Cook until done, turning often. Remove fatback. Add fresh corn, margarine, salt and pepper. Stir; add water. Cook until tender, 45 minutes to 1 hour. Keep adding water as necessary. Add flour and stir. Cook an additional 5 minutes.

Mom's Cabbage

Clear Run Farms—Harrells

1 1/2 lbs. CLEAR RUN FARMS® HICKORY SMOKED SAUSAGE
1 head of fresh CABBAGE, coarsely chopped
3 Tbsp. CLEAR RUN FARMS® PIG PICK 'N SAUCE

Slice smoked sausage into bite-size pieces and place in a large pot over medium heat. Place cabbage on top of sausage and sprinkle sauce over cabbage. Cover and let cook; stirring after 10 minutes. Let cook for 20 to 30 minutes, stirring occasionally.

Serves 3-4.

Sweet Potatoes with Streusel Topping

North Carolina SweetPotato Commission—Smithfield

2 lg. (14 to 16 oz. ea.) SWEET POTATOES
1 tsp. MARGARINE, melted

Cut sweet potatoes in half lengthwise; prick with fork. Place on paper towels with cut side up. Microwave 10 minutes, rearranging pieces after 5 minutes. Brush each half of sweet potato with 1/4 teaspoon melted margarine; fluff up and sprinkle with *Streusel Topping*. Microwave on high for 2 minutes.

Streusel Topping

1/3 cup QUICK COOKING OATS
4 tsp. chopped PECANS
2 Tbsp. BROWN SUGAR
1 Tbsp. MARGARINE

In a skillet, toast oats and pecans over medium-high heat for 3 to 4 minutes or until mixture begins to brown. Add brown sugar and margarine; cook until margarine has melted.

Serves 4.

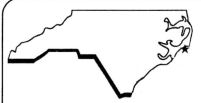

Cape Hatteras National Seashore and the Cape Hatteras Lighthouse

The Cape Hatteras National Seashore encompasses 45 square miles of the Outer Banks. This national recreation area includes Ocracoke, Hatteras and part of Bodie (Body) Islands. Crossing to the islands via a free bridge and ferry, visitors have free access to the ocean. The Cape Hatteras Lighthouse was built in 1870 and is the tallest such brick structure in the United States. The 2900-foot move of the lighthouse, to protect it from shoreline deterioration, was completed on July 9, 1999.

Old Timey Chow-Chow

"This is usually made in the fall when mountain cabbage is the best. It's wonderful with dried beans and other vegetables."

Magdalene Comer—Mount Airy

2 CABBAGES, chopped
1 gallon GREEN TOMATOES, chopped
1 peck GREEN and RED BELL PEPPERS, chopped
2 or 3 HOT PEPPERS, chopped
1 gallon ONIONS, chopped
1/2 to 2/3 cup NON-IODIZED SALT
6 cups SUGAR
6 cups VINEGAR

Mix all vegetables in a big plastic or crock container; use gloves. Add salt and mix. Let stand overnight. The next day, remove by double handfuls, squeezing out excess liquid. Put into a large stockpot, add sugar and vinegar and cook 30 minutes. Place in sterilized jars and seal according to manufacturers directions.

Did You Know?

Historians have recorded North Carolina's products during the colonial period as: tar, pitch and turpentine. One century later, during the civil war, General Lee referred to fighters in North Carolina as the Tar Heel boys, and the name stuck.

Redeye Gravy

"This gravy is commonly served with grits and homemade biscuits."

Stevens Sausage Co., Inc.—Smithfield

Sliced STEVENS® COUNTRY HAM
1/4 cup WATER

In large skillet, fry ham. After ham is fully cooked, remove from skillet. Reduce heat to medium-low. Slowly add water to drippings in pan. Cook for about 2 minutes, stirring constantly.

Breads

Tabor City Yam Bread

"The yam is celebrated annually in Tabor City, the 'Yam Capital of the World,' the fourth week of October at the North Carolina Yam Festival."

Gloria T. Rogers—Four Rooster Inn, Tabor City

6 Tbsp. BUTTER	2 tsp. BAKING POWDER
1 cup SUGAR	1/4 tsp. CLOVES
2 EGGS	1/2 tsp. NUTMEG
1 cup cooked and mashed YAMS	1/4 tsp. CINNAMON
or SWEET POTATOES	1/2 tsp. SALT
2 cups ALL-PURPOSE FLOUR	1/3-1/2 cup MILK
1/4 tsp. BAKING SODA	1/2 cup chopped NUTS

Preheat oven to 350°. Butter an 8 x 8-inch pan. In a large bowl, blend butter and sugar to a creamy consistency. Thoroughly beat in eggs; stir in mashed yams. Sift dry ingredients together and add to yam mixture, alternating with milk. Stir in nuts. Pour into pan and bake for 50-55 minutes. Top with icing if desired.

Note: This bread freezes well. It may also be baked in lined muffin tins at 400° for 15-20 minutes or, in a madeleine pan (a special pan with scallop-shell indentations) at 400° for 10 minutes.

Sweet Potato Muffins

North Carolina SweetPotato Commission—Smithfield

1 cup SUGAR
1/2 cup MARGARINE
2 EGGS
1 1/4 cups cooked, mashed SWEET POTATOES
1 1/2 cups ALL-PURPOSE FLOUR
2 tsp. BAKING POWDER
1/4 tsp. SALT
1 tsp. CINNAMON
1/4 tsp. NUTMEG
1 cup MILK
1/4 cup chopped NUTS
1/4 cup RAISINS

Preheat oven to 400°. Grease muffin tins. Cream sugar and margarine; add eggs, mixing well. Blend in sweet potatoes. Sift together flour, baking powder, salt, and spices. Add to creamed mixture alternating with milk. Fold in nuts and raisins. Fill muffin tins 1/2 full and bake for 25 minutes.

Note: Batter can be stored in the refrigerator for up to 4 days.

Plum Good Muffins

Tim Johnson—Cary

2 cups SUGAR
2 cups SELF-RISING FLOUR
1 cup OIL
3 EGGS
2 small jars PLUM BABY FOOD
2 tsp. ALLSPICE
1 cup chopped WALNUTS or PECANS

Combine and mix all ingredients. Spoon into mini-muffin pans (large muffins and loaves do not work well). Bake in preheated 325° oven for about 15 minutes. Serve with plum preserves, plum jelly and/or butter.

Cornbread & Corn Muffins

Buffaloe Milling Co., Inc—Kittrell

1/4 cup COOKING OIL or
    SHORTENING
1 1/2 cups BARTON'S®
    SELF-RISING CORNMEAL

1/2 cup SELF-RISING FLOUR
1/2 cup SUGAR
1 cup BUTTERMILK
2 EGGS

Cornbread: Preheat oven to 350°. Grease a 10-inch skillet with half of oil and warm on top of stove at medium heat. Combine the rest of oil with remaining ingredients. Blend until smooth. Pour into warm skillet and bake for 20 to 30 minutes, or until brown on top. Serve hot with butter.

Corn Muffins: Combine all ingredients and spoon into a greased muffin pan. Bake at 350° for approximately 25 minutes.

Carrot Cornbread

"Self-rising cornmeal has baking powder, soda, and salt already added by the corn miller and blended in the correct proportions for leavening."

North Carolina Corn Millers Association

2/3 cup SALAD OIL
1 cup SUGAR
2 EGGS
1 cup SELF-RISING CORNMEAL
1/2 cup SELF-RISING FLOUR
1 tsp. CINNAMON
1 1/2 cups finely grated CARROTS
3/4 cup RAISINS
1/2 cup chopped WALNUTS or PECANS

Mix together oil and sugar; add eggs. Sift flour and cornmeal; add to egg mixture. Add remaining ingredients, mixing thoroughly. Pour into a well-greased loaf pan and bake in a 350° oven for 45 to 50 minutes.

Serves 12.

Ginger Bread
with Lemon Sauce

"My mama and I have baked this bread many, many times.

Bonnie B. Lewis—Winston-Salem

1/2 cup BUTTER
3/4 cup SUGAR
2 EGGS
1 cup SOUR MILK
1 cup MOLASSES
3 cups FLOUR

2 tsp. BAKING SODA
2 tsp. CINNAMON
1 1/2 tsp. GINGER
1/4 tsp. CLOVES
1/4 tsp. ALLSPICE

In a bowl, beat butter and sugar until well creamed. Add the eggs and sour milk and beat well. Add molasses and stir until well-blended. In a separate bowl, mix remaining ingredients. Stir dry mixture into creamed mixture until just blended. Pour into a loaf pan, and bake at 350° for 20 minutes. Serve hot *Lemon Sauce* over top of bread.

Lemon Sauce

1 cup SUGAR
3 Tbsp. CORNSTARCH
2 cups boiling WATER

6 Tbsp. LEMON JUICE
2 Tbsp. grated LEMON ZEST
4 Tbsp. BUTTER

Combine sugar and cornstarch in a saucepan. Slowly add water, lemon juice and zest, while stirring constantly. Add butter and simmer over low heat, stirring constantly for 5 minutes, or until clear and thick. Serve hot over ginger bread.

Mt. Airy

Just outside of Mount Airy in Surry County is the largest open-face granite quarry in the world. It measures one mile long and 1,800 feet in width. North Carolina granite has been used for government structures throughout the United States. Granite was designated the official rock for the State of North Carolina in 1979.

Hobo Bread

"This family recipe originated with the pioneers and has been shared down through the ages. It may be served as either bread or cake."

Geraldine Mayo Beveridge—Beaufort

1 cup BOILING WATER
1 cup RAISINS
2 tsp. BAKING SODA
2 cups ALL-PURPOSE FLOUR
1 cup SUGAR
3 Tbsp. OIL
Pinch of SALT (optional)

Pour water over raisins. Add baking soda. Let soak until cool, about 1 hour. Mix together the remaining ingredients; add the raisin mixture. Pour into a greased 5 x 9 loaf pan. Bake at 350° for about one hour.

Note: Pecans, walnuts or dried fruits may be added.

Squash Muffins

Tar Heel Kitchen—North Carolina Department of Agriculture and Consumer Services, Raleigh

1 EGG
1 cup LOW-FAT MILK
2/3 cup grated YELLOW SQUASH
2 cups ALL-PURPOSE FLOUR
1 Tbsp. BAKING POWDER
1/4 tsp. SALT
1/2 cup SUGAR
2 Tbsp. VEGETABLE OIL

Beat egg in a medium mixing bowl; add milk and squash. Combine dry ingredients; stir into squash mixture. Stir in oil. Grease muffin tins. Heat oven to 350°, or, heat tins and then place paper liners in cups. Spoon batter into tins, filling cups two-thirds full. Bake about 20 minutes or until done.

Makes one dozen muffins.

Pumpkin Bread

"This is one of my grandchildren's favorites."

Stella Hutchens—Yadkinville

2 cups cooked PUMPKIN
1 cup OIL
3 cups SUGAR
3 1/2 cups ALL-PURPOSE FLOUR
1/2 tsp. NUTMEG
1/2 tsp. CINNAMON
2 tsp. SALT
4 EGGS

Mix all together, blending thoroughly. Pour into 2 greased and floured loaf pans. Bake at 350° until brown and a toothpick inserted in middle comes out clean.

Orange Poppy Seed Bread

"This is a long standing favorite among our guests."

Donna Black & Nancy Caviness—Proprietors; Advice 5¢, a bed & breakfast, Duck

2 cups ALL-PURPOSE FLOUR
2 tsp. BAKING POWDER
1/2 tsp. SALT
1/3 cup POPPY SEEDS
1/2 cup BUTTER, softened
1 cup SUGAR
2 lg. EGGS
1 cup MILK
1 tsp. pure VANILLA EXTRACT
1/2 tsp. pure ORANGE EXTRACT
1/2 tsp. pure ALMOND EXTRACT
grated ZEST of 1 med. ORANGE

Preheat oven to 350°. Coat one loaf pan with vegetable spray. Mix together dry ingredients. Using an electric mixer, cream butter and sugar for 3 minutes or until light and fluffy; beat in eggs (one at a time). Add milk, extracts, and zest. On low speed, slowly blend dry ingredients to liquid mixture until just combined. Do not over-mix! Spoon batter into loaf pan, smoothing on top. Bake for 1 hour and 15 minutes, or until tester comes out clean. Allow to cool in pan for 10 minutes before removing from pan to cooling rack. Cool completely before slicing.

North Carolina Persimmon Pudding

"My father would tell stories that his father told him about Civil War soldiers who, having little to eat, would always be happy to find persimmon trees as they began to ripen in the fall. This pudding is one of the oldest recipes in North Carolina."

Shelby Cannon—Asheboro

3 cups SUGAR
3 cups FLOUR
3 cups PERSIMMON PULP
2 cups SWEET MILK
4 EGGS
1 cup BUTTERMILK

3/4 cup BUTTER
1 tsp. BAKING SODA
1 tsp. CINNAMON
1 tsp. NUTMEG
2 tsp. VANILLA

Cream sugar, flour, and persimmon pulp. Add sweet milk and blend well; then add eggs, one at a time, beating well after each addition. Mix in remaining ingredients. Pour into 9 x 13 baking pan and bake at 325° for 1 1/2 hours.

Hummingbird Cake

*This cake, made with fruits and nuts, is said to be sweet
enough to attract hummingbirds.*

2 cups FLOUR
1 1/2 cups SUGAR
1/4 tsp. SALT
2 tsp. BAKING POWDER
1 tsp. CINNAMON
3 lg. EGGS, beaten
1 cup OIL
2 tsp. VANILLA
1 can (8 oz.) CRUSHED PINEAPPLE, undrained
3 med. BANANAS, coarsely mashed
1 1/2 cups chopped PECANS

Pre-heat oven to 350°. Grease and flour 2 (9-inch) cake
pans. Combine dry ingredients in a large bowl. Stir in eggs, oil
and vanilla, blending well. Add pineapple, banana and pecans.
Spoon batter into prepared pans. Bake 25 to 35 minutes, or
until a wooden pick inserted in center comes out clean. Cool on
wire rack for 15 minutes, then remove cakes from pan. Cool
cakes completely on a wire rack before frosting with ***Cream
Cheese Frosting.***

Cream Cheese Frosting

1 stick BUTTER
1 pkg. (8 oz.) CREAM CHEESE, softened
1 1/2 tsp. VANILLA
1 pkg. (1 lb.) POWDERED SUGAR, sifted

Cream butter and cream cheese; add vanilla, mixing well.
Add confectioners sugar, beat until fluffy.

The Blue Ridge Parkway

*This parkway, which at times is only 800 feet wide, is 469
miles long. It stretches from west of Asheville in the western
part of the state and travels northeast across the Blue Ridge
Mountains and continues into Virginia.*

Old Fashioned Stack Cake

"I am 83-years-old and my mother made this cake when I was growing up. She used lard, as that was the only cooking grease she had."

Pearl Misenheimer—Yadkinville

1/2 cup SHORTENING
1 cup firmly packed BROWN SUGAR
1/2 cup MOLASSES
2 EGGS
3 cups ALL-PURPOSE FLOUR
1 tsp. BAKING POWDER
1 tsp. SALT
1/2 tsp. ground CINNAMON
1/2 tsp. ground GINGER

Combine shortening, sugar, molasses and eggs; cream until light and fluffy. Combine remaining ingredients and add to creamed mixture, blending well. Cover and chill at least 1 hour. Divide dough into five parts and pat each into well greased and floured 9-inch cake pans. Bake at 350° for 8 to 10 minutes. While warm, spread *Apple Filling* over top.

Apple Filling

1 lb. dried APPLES
1 1/2 cups firmly packed BROWN SUGAR
3/4 cup WHITE SUGAR
2 tsp. ground CINNAMON

Cover apples with water and cook until tender, about 30 minutes. While apples are hot, add the sugars and cinnamon and stir until well blended. Spread filling on each of the five cake layers as you stack them.

Swiss Apple Torte

"My grandmother, Mary Leah Elizabeth Overcash Sloan, wrote this recipe many years ago. We have her original copy. My mother, Faye Washam Sloan, recalls that it started out as cake layers instead of cookie-like layers, but because of a mistake my grandmother made when she prepared it one time, we found that we preferred the new style."

Madelyn Sloan Hill—Madelyn's in the Grove, Union Grove

Cake:

1 stick BUTTER, softened	1 1/2 cups SUGAR
3 EGG YOLKS	3 cups FLOUR
3 Tbsp. MILK	1/8 tsp. SALT
1 tsp. VANILLA	1 tsp. BAKING POWDER

Preheat oven to 325°. Spray 3 (9-inch) cake pans with vegetable spray, dust with flour, and line with parchment or wax paper. Combine butter, egg yolks, milk and vanilla. Add sugar and blend well. Sift flour, salt and baking powder into the mixture, stirring until all ingredients are well blended. The batter will be very stiff. Divide dough into 3 equal parts and spread dough in each pan by patting with fingertips. Bake for 25 to 30 minutes or until lightly brown. Cool on wire racks. To assemble, place one cake layer on a parchment-lined cookie sheet. Spread with half of **Apple Filling**. Repeat with second layer and remaining filling. Top with third layer. Ice cake with **Meringue Topping**. Bake for 10 to 12 minutes or until golden brown. Transfer to a serving plate.

Note: Cake is best if made one day before serving. Keep refrigerated.

(Continued on next page)

Apple Filling

1 1/2 cups SUGAR
1/2 tsp. CINNAMON
1/2 cup APPLE JUICE
2 lbs. GRANNY SMITH APPLES, peeled, cored and thinly sliced

In a 2-quart saucepan, bring sugar, cinnamon, and apple juice to a boil. Slowly drop apple slices into boiling juice mixture. Reduce heat and simmer until liquid is absorbed (45 minutes to an hour).

Meringue Topping

3 EGG WHITES   6 Tbsp. SUGAR

Beat egg whites with sugar until stiff peaks form.

Pound Cake

"This recipe has been in my family for 38 years."

Gretchen Rhodes—Madison

3 sticks BUTTER   1/2 tsp. SALT
1/2 cup CRISCO®   3 cups FLOUR
3 cups SUGAR   1 cup MILK
5 EGGS   2 tsp. LEMON FLAVORING
1/2 tsp. BAKING POWDER   1 tsp. VANILLA FLAVORING

Cream butter, Crisco, and sugar together. Add eggs, one at a time, beating thoroughly after each addition. Stir in baking powder and salt. Add flour and milk; beat well, then add flavorings. Pour into a greased and lightly floured tube pan. Bake at 350° for 1 1/2 hours.

Sweet Potato Cake

North Carolina SweetPotato Commission—Smithfield

1 can (20 oz.) sliced PINEAPPLE in natural juice
1 Tbsp. BUTTER
1/4 cup packed LIGHT BROWN SUGAR
1 tsp. ground GINGER
1/4 cup dried CRANBERRIES
1 pkg. (14 1/2 oz.) GINGERBREAD CAKE MIX
2 EGGS
1 1/2 cups peeled and grated SWEET POTATOES

Drain pineapple; reserving 1/2 cup plus 3 tablespoonsful of the juice. Set aside 1 whole pineapple slice. Cut 5 slices in half. (saving remainder for another use.) Preheat oven to 350°. Put butter in a 9-inch round cake pan and place in the oven until butter melts; set aside. In a small bowl, combine brown sugar, ginger, and the 3 tablespoons of pineapple juice. Pour mixture into pan with melted butter and tilt to evenly distribute. Place whole pineapple ring in center of the pan; arrange half slices in crescents around the center. Fill in spaces with dried cranberries. In a bowl, combine dry cake mix, eggs, sweet potatoes, and 1/2 cup pineapple juice. Using a fork, stir vigorously about 2 minutes, scraping sides until well mixed. Spread over pineapple in pan. Bake 45 to 50 minutes or until a wooden pick inserted in center comes out clean. Cool 5 minutes; invert on platter. Serve warm or at room temperature.

Serves 8-10.

High Point

When is a chest of drawers not just a chest of drawers? When it is a 40 foot tall office building and headquarters of the High Point Jaycees! High Point, known as the Furnishings Capital of the World, hosts the International Home Furnishings Market trade show in April and October.

Grandview Chocolate Tart

"This is probably my most requested recipe. If you're a chocoholic, like I am, you're going to love it."

Linda P. Arnold—Grandview Lodge, Waynesville

Crust:
   1 3/4 cups FLOUR
   1/3 cup COCOA
   1/4 cup SUGAR
   1/4 cup SHORTENING
   1/2 cup BUTTER or MARGARINE
   1/3-1/2 cup ICE WATER
Filling:
   12 oz. BITTERSWEET or SEMI-SWEET CHOCOLATE CHIPS
   2/3 cup SUGAR
   1 Tbsp. CHOCOLATE or COFFEE LIQUEUR
   1 Tbsp. INSTANT COFFEE POWDER
   2 Tbsp. MILK
   2 EGGS
   1 cup coarsely chopped WALNUTS

In a large mixing bowl, combine first three ingredients. Using a pastry blender or 2 knives, cut shortening and butter into flour mixture until it resembles coarse meal. Add water slowly, mixing with a fork. Add only enough water to gather into a ball. Wrap in plastic wrap and chill. This dough is stickier than ordinary pie pastry. Roll out between 2 pieces of floured wax paper. Line an 11-inch spring-form pan with the pastry. In the top of a double boiler or in a heavy saucepan, melt chocolate. Stir in remaining ingredients except nuts. Pour mixture into prepared pastry. Sprinkle with nuts. Bake in preheated 375° oven for 30-35 minutes or until set in center. Filling will puff up slightly and crack. Cool on a wire rack. Remove sides of pan. Cut and serve.

Serves 12-16.

Susan's Pecan Pie Rx

Susan Johnson—Cary

3 EGGS
1/2 cup SUGAR
1 cup DARK CORN SYRUP
1/3 cup melted BUTTER
1/2 lb. chopped or crushed PECANS
1 (9-inch) unbaked PASTRY SHELL

Beat eggs thoroughly with sugar, corn syrup and butter. Add pecans. Pour into pastry shell. Bake at 350° for about 50 minutes, or until knife inserted halfway between outside and center of filling comes out clean.

Sweet Potato Pudding

North Carolina SweetPotato Commission—Smithfield

2 cups cooked, mashed SWEET POTATOES
1/2 cup firmly packed BROWN SUGAR
3 Tbsp. MARGARINE, melted
2 EGGS, separated
3/4 cup unsweetened ORANGE JUICE
1/4 tsp. ground NUTMEG
1/4 tsp. ground CLOVES
Dash of SALT
2 Tbsp. SUGAR

Combine potatoes, brown sugar, margarine and egg yolks in a large bowl. Gradually add orange juice, nutmeg and cloves; stir well. Set aside. Beat egg whites until foamy; add salt and beat until soft peaks form. Fold egg whites into potato mixture. Pour mixture into a 1 1/2-quart baking dish coated with cooking spray. Place baking dish in a large, shallow pan, adding hot water in pan to a depth of 1 inch. Bake at 350° for 1 hour or until center is set and edges are browned. Remove dish from water; let cool 15 minutes before serving.

Serves 8-10.

Tea Cakes

"My husband's grandmother, Nina Medford McCarter, grew up living over the jail in Madison County (her father was the sheriff). Occasionally, she would even take meals down to the prisoners. My mother-in-law, Dot Hampton, credits her grandmother's cookbook, which means the sheriff of Madison County could have enjoyed these tea cakes too."

Jan Hampton—Winston-Salem

1/2 cup BUTTER or MARGARINE	2 tsp. BAKING POWDER
1 cup SUGAR	3 cups FLOUR
2 EGGS, beaten	1 tsp. VANILLA
2 Tbsp. MILK	1/4 tsp. MACE

Cream butter; add sugar, eggs, and milk. Mix in dry ingredients. Roll dough on a floured surface to desired thickness, adding flour as needed. Cut with cookie cutters. Bake at 350° for 10 to 12 minutes or until light brown.

Camp Lejeune

Established in 1941, Camp Lejeune serves as a home base and training center for a combat division and force troops of the U.S. Fleet Marine Forces, Atlantic. It covers 83,000 acres and has the largest naval hospital in the South.

Baked Cinnamon Apples

North Carolina Apple Growers Association—Edneyville

4 BAKING APPLES	4 tsp. BUTTER
1/2 cup packed BROWN SUGAR	1/2 tsp. CINNAMON

Remove core from apples. Peel upper half of apple or 1-inch strip from middle to prevent splitting. Place apples upright in baking dish. Place 2 tablespoons brown sugar, 1 teaspoon butter and 1/8 teaspoon cinnamon in center of each apple. Pour water into baking dish to 1/4-inch depth. Bake at 375° for 30-40 minutes or until tender. Baste several times during baking.

Sweet Potato Pie

Tar Heel Kitchen—North Carolina Department of Agriculture and Consumer Services, Raleigh

1 (9-inch) unbaked PIE CRUST
2 cups mashed cooked SWEET POTATOES
1 cup firmly packed BROWN SUGAR
1/2 stick BUTTER, melted
2 EGGS, beaten
1 cup HALF & HALF
1 tsp. CINNAMON
1/2 tsp. ALLSPICE
1 Tbsp. LEMON JUICE

Heat oven to 400°. Bake crust for 15 minutes. Reduce oven heat to 350°. In a large bowl, blend sweet potatoes with sugar; add melted butter, mixing well. Mix in eggs and half & half. Add remaining ingredients, blending well. Pour into pie crust. Bake 30 to 40 minutes or until pie is set.

Orange Pie

"This recipe has been in my family for years."

Eva Tuttle—Winston-Salem

1 (9-inch) unbaked PASTRY SHELL
3 EGG YOLKS
1/4 cup plus 6 Tbsp. SUGAR
Grated rind and juice of 1 ORANGE
Grated rind and juice of 1 LEMON
1 Tbsp. BUTTER, melted
3 EGG WHITES
1 Tbsp. ORANGE JUICE

Whip egg yolks with 1/4 cup sugar; add orange and lemon rinds and juice, and butter. Mix thoroughly. Pour into pastry shell. Bake for 10 minutes in a 400° oven, reduce heat to 350° and bake 35 minutes longer, or until set. Beat egg whites with 6 tablespoons sugar, adding orange juice just before beating the last time. Spread over pie. Bake in a 300° oven for 15 minutes, or until golden brown.

Coconut Pie

Gretchen Rhodes—Madison

3/4 cup SUGAR
2 Tbsp. FLOUR
3 EGG YOLKS
2 cups MILK

1 pkg. (7 oz.) COCONUT FLAKES
1 tsp. VANILLA FLAVORING
1 (9-inch) baked PIE CRUST

Mix sugar, flour and egg yolks in a saucepan. Gradually add milk, stirring until smooth. Cook over low heat, stirring often, until mixture has thickened. Remove from heat and add coconut (reserve some for topping) and vanilla. Mix well. Pour into pie crust. Spread *Coconut Pie Topping* over top of pie and sprinkle with reserved coconut. Bake at 350° approximately 10 minutes or until topping is golden brown.

Coconut Pie Topping

3 EGG WHITES
dash of SALT
6 Tbsp. SUGAR

Beat egg whites with salt until stiff, adding sugar gradually. Continue to beat until meringue holds its shape.

Blue Ribbon Grated Apple Pie

North Carolina Apple Growers Association—Edneyville

1 stick BUTTER or MARGARINE
1 cup SUGAR
1 large EGG, beaten
1/2 tsp. CINNAMON
Dash of NUTMEG and/or GINGER
2 1/2 cups shredded APPLES, drained
1 (9-inch) unbaked PIE CRUST

Mix first six ingredients together and fill pie crust. Bake at 350° for 1 hour.

Serves 6-8.

Peanut Butter Pie

"My mother used to make this when I was a child. I made it for my children and now I make it for my grandchildren. Everyone loves it."

Barbara McDonald—Winston-Salem

2 cups CHUNKY PEANUT BUTTER
2 (8-inch) baked PIE SHELLS
1 pkg. (8 oz.) CREAM CHEESE, softened
3/4 cup POWDERED SUGAR
1 cup CREAMY PEANUT BUTTER
2 Tbsp. PLAIN GELATIN
1/4 cup BOILING WATER
1/4 cup MILK
1 tsp. VANILLA
1 ctn. (16 oz.) WHIPPED TOPPING
1/4 cup CHOCOLATE SYRUP
1/2 cup chopped PEANUTS

Spread chunky peanut butter in bottom of both pie shells. Beat cream cheese, sugar, and creamy peanut butter together until thoroughly combined. Dissolve gelatin in boiling water and add to cream cheese mixture. Add milk and vanilla and mix until smooth. Gently fold in whipped topping until thoroughly mixed. Spread over chunky peanut butter in pie shells. Freeze for at least 1 hour. Take out of freezer and let thaw for 20 minutes before serving. Stripe the pie with chocolate syrup and sprinkle with chopped nuts.

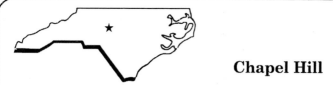

Chapel Hill

Named for the New Hope Chapel which was erected on a hill denoting the crossing of two main roads, this community is now the home of the University of North Carolina at Chapel Hill. Chartered in 1789, this was the first university in the United States to accept and graduate students.

Malted Cheesecake Ice Cream with Peanut Butter Cups

"When my roommate ate some of my ice cream ingredients, I couldn't make the two flavors I had planned. So I combined two recipes together for this one."

Vaughn Jett—Durham

6 cups MILK
1 pt. HEAVY CREAM
1 cup SUGAR or more,
    to taste
2 tsp. VANILLA
1 tsp. LEMON JUICE
2 tsp. CINNAMON

1 cup MALTED MILK POWDER
1 pkg. (16 oz.) SOUR CREAM
1 pkg. (8 oz.) CREAM CHEESE,
    softened
12 REESES'S® PEANUT BUTTER
    CUPS, coarsely chopped

In a large bowl or food processor, blend all ingredients except peanut butter cups until smooth. Taste; add more sugar if desired. Stir in peanut butter cups. Pour into ice cream freezer and follow manufacturer's directions to freeze.

Kitty Hawk

On December 17, 1903, near Kitty Hawk, Orville and Wilbur Wright tested and flew the world's first power-driven, heavier-than-air machine. Orville was the pilot for that flight. The same day, the Wrights flew three flights with Wilbur piloting the longest—852 feet.

Apple Dip

North Carolina Apple Growers Association—Edneyville

1 pkg. (8 oz.) CREAM CHEESE, softened
1/4 cup ORANGE JUICE CONCENTRATE
1 Tbsp. ORANGE PEEL
1 jar (7 oz.) MARSHMALLOW CREAM

Mix cream cheese with orange juice concentrate; add orange peel. Add marshmallow cream and place in refrigerator until ready to use. Serve with apple wedges.

Taffy-Apple Dip

North Carolina Apple Growers Association—Edneyville

1 pkg. (8 oz.) CREAM CHEESE, softened
3/4 cup firmly packed BROWN SUGAR
1 Tbsp. VANILLA

Mix cream cheese with sugar; add vanilla. Refrigerate until ready to use. Serve with apple wedges.

The Tar Heel Toast

The following toast was officially adopted as the State Toast of North Carolina by the General Assembly of 1957.

Here's to the land of the long leaf pine,
The summer land where the sun doth shine
Where the weak grow strong and the strong grow great,
Here's to "Down Home," the Old North State!

Here's to the land of the cotton bloom white,
Where the scuppernong perfumes the breeze at night,
Where the soft southern moss and jessamine mate,
'Neath the murmuring pines of the Old North State!

Here's to the land where the galax grows,
Where the rhododendron's rosette glows,
Where soars Mount Mitchell's summit great,
In the "Land of the Sky," in the Old North State!

Here's to the land where maidens are fair,
Where friends are true and cold hearts rare,
The near land, the dear land, whatever fate,
The blest land, the best land, the Old North State!

Index

Index (continued)

Index (continued)

Index (continued)

Recipe Contributors

About the Author

Janice Therese Mancuso is also the author of "Herbed-Wine Cuisine, Creating and Cooking with Herb Infused Wines." She owns a specialty food company, develops recipes for food manufacturers and is a cooking instructor. She publishes "Simply Elegant", a quarterly newsletter on food, decorating, and entertaining; writes a monthly on-line column for the MyCookbook web site, and writes for various food publications.

Visit Janice's web site: www.jtmancuso.com.

Product Resource Guide

Animal John's Southern Food
5119A New Hope Road, Apt. 2
Raleigh, NC 27604 (919-954-0150)
Animal John's All-Purpose Southern Sauce

Anne's Old Fashioned Food Products
3857 Emma Cannon Road
Ayden, NC 28513 (888-291-9097)
Anne's Old Fashioned Flat Dumplings and
Chicken Base

Buffaloe Milling Company, Inc.
P.O. Box 145
Kittrell, NC 27544 (252-438-8637)
Barton's Self-Rising Cornmeal

Carolina Classics Catfish, Inc.,
P.O. Box 10
Ayden, NC 28513 (252-746-2818)
Classics Catfish Fillets

Carolina Treet, Inc.
814 North Third Street
Wilmington, NC 28402 (910-762-1950)
Carolina Treet Barbecue Sauce

Carolina Turkeys
P.O. Box 589
Mt. Olive, NC 28365 (800-523-4559)
Carolina Turkey Breasts

Clear Run Farms
P.O. Box 109
Harrells, NC 28444 (800-863-7619)
Clear Run Farms Pig Pick 'N Sauce
and *Hickory Smoked Sausage*

Dixie Trail Farms, Inc.,
1939-197 High House Road
Cary, NC 27513 (800-665-3869)
Dixie Trail Farms Special Spice

Duplin Winery
P.O. Box 756, Hwy. 117
Rose Hill, NC 28458 (800-774-9634)
Scuppernong Wine

Eloras Exquisite Foods
P.O. Box 37173
Raleigh, NC 27627 (919-233-9443)
Eloras Tamarind Fruit Sauce

House-Autry Mills, Inc.
635 House Mill Road
Newton Grove, NC 28366-0040 (910-594-0802)
Hause-Autry Hushpuppy Mix and *Seafood
Breader*

Mt. Olive Pickle Company
P.O. Box 1295
Mt. Olive, NC 28053 (704-865-1137)
Sweet Pickled Red and *Cherry Peppers*

Neese Country Sausage
1452 Alamance Church Road
Greensboro, NC 27406 (800-632-1010)
Neese's Sausage (regular, hot, or sage)

Old Waynesboro Country Ham
Wayco Ham Company Corp.
508 N. William Street
Goldsboro, NC 27530 (800-962-2614)
Old Waynesboro Country Ham

Pantego Plantation Gourmet Foods
P.O. Box 279
Pantego, NC 27860 (252-943-6182)
Pantego Plantation Breader

Ragsdale-Overton Food Traditions
P.O. Box 1626
Smithfield, NC 27577 (919-284-6700)
Raggy-O Chutneys

Stevens Sausage Co., Inc.,
P.O. Box 2304
Smithfield, NC 27577 (800-338-0561)
Steven's Country Ham

Thomas Gourmet Foods
P.O. Box 8822
Greensboro, NC 27419 (910-299-6263)
Thomas Sauce

T&K Sauces, Inc.
377 Pearson Circle
Newport, NC 28570 (919-393-6990)
Shipwreck Sauce

TW Garner Food Company
P.O. Box 4329
Winston-Salem, NC 27115
(336-661-1550)
*Garner's Pineapple Preserves, Texas
Pete Honey Mustard* and *Hot Sauces*

Watauga Country Ham
P.O. Box 287
Boone, NC 28607 (828-264-8892)
Watauga Country Ham

Web Sauce Foods
P.O. Box 77596
Greensboro, NC 27417 (336-294-1441)
Web Sauce

If you love cookbooks, then you'll love these too!

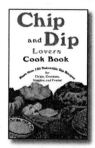

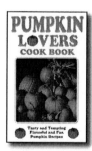

QTY	TITLE	PRICE	TOTAL
	Burrito Lovers' Cook Book	9.95	
	Chili Lovers' Cook Book	9.95	
	Chip & Dip Lovers' Cook Book	9.95	
	Citrus Lovers' Cook Book	9.95	
	Easy BBQ Recipes	9.95	
	Easy BBQ Sauces	9.95	
	Grand Canyon Cook Book	9.95	
	Low Fat Mexican Recipes	9.95	
	New Mexico Cook Book	9.95	
	Mexican Family Favorites Cook Book	9.95	
	Quick-n-Easy Mexican Recipes	9.95	
	Salsa Lovers' Cook Book	9.95	
	Sedona Cook Book	9.95	
	Tequila Cook Book	9.95	
	Texas Cook Book	9.95	
	Tortilla Lovers' Cook Book	9.95	
	Veggie Lovers' Cook Book	9.95	
	Western Breakfast	9.95	

US Shipping & Handling Add	1-3 Books: 5.00	
[for non-domestic ship rates, please call]	4-9 Books: 7.00	
	9+ Books: 7.00 + 0.25 per book	
	AZ residents add 8.1% sales tax	

(US funds only) Total:

Please make checks payable to:
Golden West Publishers
4113 N. Longview,
Phoenix, AZ 85014

☐ Check or money order enclosed
☐ MC   ☐ VISA   ☐ Discover   ☐ American Express   Verification Code:_____

Card Number:_____ Exp._____

Signature: _____

Name_____Phone:_____

Address _____

City_____State_____ZIP _____

Email _____

Prices are subject to change.

Visit our website or call us toll free for a free catalog of all our titles!